VIRGINIA
LEGENDS & LORE

VIRGINIA
LEGENDS & LORE

CHARLES A. MILLS

THE
History
PRESS

Published by The History Press
Charleston, SC
www.historypress.com

All images courtesy of the Library of Congress unless otherwise noted.

First published 2021

Manufactured in the United States

ISBN 9781467149709

Library of Congress Control Number: 2021938367

Notice: The information in this book is true and complete to the best of our knowledge. It is offered without guarantee on the part of the author or The History Press. The author and The History Press disclaim all liability in connection with the use of this book.

For Gracie

CONTENTS

Contents

PREFACE

W hy do people hate history but love stories based on history? There was a historical King Arthur; he was a Roman-British warlord who resisted the barbarian invasions as the Roman Empire collapsed in Britain. The dates usually attributed to King Arthur lie between AD 460 and 540. What people are really interested in, however, is not the flesh-and-blood man, but tales of the Knights of the Roundtable and the Quest for the Holy Grail. The Arthurian legend, like all great legends, encompasses the great things of life: courage, love, duty, loyalty, human frailty, compassion, redemption and the hope of enlightenment. Who cares about a few facts and dates compared to these things?

A people's legends and lore are those sweet, mysterious, alluring stories of heroes and villains; of things strange and wonderful; those stories that, if they are not true, should be. For centuries, Virginians have told and retold, created and embellished wonderful stories of their history. These stories tug at our imaginations; these are the things of which dreams are made. So here we present for your consideration the often-overlooked stories of Virginia from pre-colonial times to modern times. Included are stories such as the wild Spanish ponies of Chincoteague, General Braddock's lost gold, the Mount Vernon Monster and the Richmond Vampire. Here we explore secret societies and hidden knowledge, like the Bruton Parish Mystery, and delve into the mysteries of the universe as we pursue one of the most famous UFO sightings in American history. And then there are the people—stories of Revolutionary War heroes, Annandale's "bunny man" who inspired one of the wildest and scariest urban legends, a slave who became a Union spy in the White House of the Confederacy and many other folks who have left their imprint on the Commonwealth of Virginia and the nation.

Many fine storytellers and history enthusiasts have shared their insights and knowledge with me. I want to especially thank my son, Andrew L. Mills, a consummate storyteller with a true passion for history; Eric Buckland, Don Hakenson and Chuck Mauro, the go-to guys for all things connected with the Civil War; Dennis VanDerlaske for his knowledge of railroad lore; Kim Murphy for making me aware of Virginia's witch trials; Walt "AZ" Guenther, the go-to guy for all things strange and wonderful; Billy Willard for his firsthand accounts of Bigfoot; Paula Kirby for her accounts of Civil War ghosts; Marion Meany; and Mary Lipsey.

NATIVE AMERICAN LEGENDS AND LORE

LEGENDS OF
THE GREAT DISMAL SWAMP

One of Virginia's most spectacular natural wonders is the Great Dismal Swamp, an expanse of forests, swamps and water that once spread over two thousand square miles. Today, the Great Dismal Swamp is a 107,000-acre National Wildlife Refuge in southeastern Virginia (which also overlaps three counties in North Carolina). The 3,100-acre Lake Drummond, one of only two natural lakes in Virginia, is located here. The Chesapeake, Nansemond, Chowan and Warrasqueoc tribes lived in the area at the time of the arrival of Europeans. The tribes shared the swamp for hunting and fishing. Although the main villages remained on the borders of the swamp, hunting and fishing camps were set up within the swamp. Strange legends grew about the mysterious swamp, and these were passed down from generation to generation in tribal oral traditions.

There were many strange things to explain—for example, the mysterious lights that hovered about the swamp. Today, we know these lights to be foxfire, a glowing fungi emanating from swamp gases, but in Native American mythology, these were explained as the spirits of nature, ghosts and witches.

One legend explaining the creation of Lake Drummond tells of the great and terrible Firebird. The Firebird's eyes glowed red like flames. It lived deep in the swamp and singed the tops of the trees as it flew in search of prey. Nothing was safe from the monster, which would sweep down to snatch men, women and children to take back to its hideous, blood-soaked nest.

Two tribes, traditional enemies, found themselves united because of the Firebird. The enemies hated each other, but they feared and hated the Firebird even more and knew that they must form an alliance to fight the monster. This was a straightforward enough story—except for the romantic complications that ensued. A handsome warrior named Big Bear fell in love with the beautiful maiden White Swan from the opposite tribe. White Swan loved Big Bear too but was already promised to a loathsome warrior known as Old Cold Heart.

White Swan and Big Bear went into the swamp to seek help from the Swamp Spirit, the good and gracious protector of the swamp and all living things within it. They found the Swamp Spirit, which appeared to them in the shape of a cypress tree that belched smoke (much like the great and powerful Wizard of Oz). The young lovers implored the spirit to find a way for them to be together. The Swamp Spirit agreed, but there was a price. The couple must give the Swamp Spirit their firstborn child. Just as the couple agreed to this condition, the Firebird appeared overhead.

Big Bear and White Swan ran, but the Firebird was quick. The monster snatched Big Bear in its beak and lifted him into the air. White Swan ran after them and would certainly have lost them had the Swamp Spirit not helped her to fly. At this point, Big Bear wriggled free from the monster's beak and fell to earth—smack into the middle of the bird's giant nest. The nest was full of the bones of the bird's previous victims. It also contained seven hungry baby birds ready to devour Big Bear.

White Swan diverted the Firebird's attention, darting and weaving through the sky, while Big Bear killed the seven ravenous baby firebirds. At this point, White Swan swooped down to save Big Bear. Then the voice of the great and powerful Swamp Spirit echoed through the swamp: "The Firebird knows she cannot live in this swamp as long as we have such brave people here." The Firebird made its exit, stopping only long enough to snatch up Old Cold Heart.

In the years that followed, the Firebird's great nest filled with water, forming what is now known as Lake Drummond. Big Bear and White Swan gave their firstborn over to the care of the Swamp Spirit, which turned the child into a white-tailed deer that protects the forest and leads hunters to safety.

Another legend tells the sad story of a beautiful maiden who died just before her wedding day. At night, the maiden paddles a ghostly white canoe across the tea-colored waters of Lake Drummond. In 1803, the Irish poet Thomas Moore added to the lore of the Great Dismal Swamp by adding on to the legend of the ghostly canoe. In his poem "The Lake of Dismal Swamp," Moore tells how the maiden's lover searches for the ghost canoe in the swamp but never returns, rejoining his beloved on the other side of death. To this day, people claim to see the ghost canoe plying the waters of Lake Drummond at night.

NATURAL BRIDGE

Geologists tell us that Natural Bridge, a natural stone arch that spans a ninety-foot gorge in Rockbridge County, was carved by an underground river during the Ordovician Period some 470 million years ago. Natural Bridge represents the only lasting remains of the roof of a cave through which the underground river once flowed. Today, the "Lost River," just upstream from Natural Bridge, is a perfect modern example of an underground river. The Lost River flows under a mountainside. No one knows where this stream comes from or where it finally ends up. Colored dyes and flotation devices of all types have failed to determine the source and final destination of this mysterious subterranean river. It is a genuine curiosity.

While geologists provided a good scientific explanation for the creation of Natural Bridge, often referred to as the "Eighth Wonder of the World," Native Americans had a more colorful explanation. The Monacan tribe migrated to Virginia 1,500 years ago and began constructing their villages along the broad flood plains of the James River and its tributaries, from present-day Richmond west into southwestern Virginia. The Monacans fell afoul of the warlike Shawnee and Powhatan tribes and were pursued relentlessly by their enemies. The Monacans fled into a strange forest and suddenly came to a dead end. They were confronted by a deep chasm with steep rock walls. It was a long way down to a swiftly running river. There appeared to be no way around the chasm and no way to get across the one-hundred-foot gap. In despair, the Monacans prayed to the Great Spirit for

The Great Spirit created Natural Bridge to save the Monacan tribe. They called it the "Bridge of God."

help. And then there was a great miracle. The Great Spirit answered the prayers of the people and built a bridge across the great chasm. One not so brave warrior, with little faith, suggested that the women and children be sent across the bridge first to test its reliability. If they made it, it would be safe for the menfolk to cross over. The women and children made it across safely and found shelter in a thick forest on the other side. Before the men could get across, however, the pursuing enemy were on the Monacan warriors. Convinced now that God was clearly on their side, the Monacan warriors found their courage, stood their ground on the bridge, faced the enemy and won a stunning victory. Henceforth, they referred to this place as the "Bridge of God."

The dimensions noted in the Monacan story, "high and wide," fit Natural Bridge accurately. The formation is 215 feet high and 90 feet wide. Chester Reeds first measured the bridge sitting in a special one-man basket lowered down the stone cliffs by rope.

Supposedly, George Washington surveyed the site in 1750 and carved his initials on the wall of the bridge some twenty-three feet up. Legend also says that George Washington threw a rock from the bottom of the gorge over the bridge. In 1927, a large stone was found engraved "G.W." and bearing a surveyor's cross, which is generally accepted as proof that Washington surveyed the bridge.

POWHATAN LEGENDS

People have lived in Virginia for at least twelve thousand years. At the time of first contact with Europeans, there were some fifty thousand Native Americans in Virginia divided into three language groups. The Powhatan tribe, part of the Algonquian language group, dominated eastern Virginia. The region was home to some fifteen thousand people living in two hundred villages along the rivers. At the time of the founding of Jamestown in 1607, a chief named Wahunsunacawh (called by the English "Chief Powhatan") had affiliated thirty neighboring tribes into a powerful confederation.

Storytelling was an important part of daily life. Stories explained the nature of the cosmos in terms of the plants and animals familiar to the people. Take, for example, Michabo, the Great Hare, who was the creator of the world. Michabo was the chief of all the animals, and in ancient times, he created man from dead animals, thus accounting for the tribe's close feeling of kinship to the animal world. In his journeys over the earth, Michabo destroyed monsters that would have threatened the people. One of the monsters was the Great Horned Serpent. The fossilized remains of gigantic prehistoric creatures that were sometimes found gave testament to the one-time existence of the monsters that Michabo destroyed.

Michabo placed the four winds in charge of the four corners of the earth. There was one in each region to ensure the welfare of humankind. The spirit in the east ensures that the sun starts on its daily journey. The spirit of the south supplies warmth, heat and moisture, allowing the growth of corn,

An early map of the Virginia colony includes the Powhatan tribe.

beans and squash that feed the people. The spirit in the west sends cooling and life-giving rain. The spirit of the north provides snow, allowing for the successful tracking of animals.

The legend of the "Three Sisters" was a popular story. There was once a family of five: a mother, father and three daughters. The eldest daughter was tall with long, silky hair. The youngest daughter was small but muscular. The middle daughter was very average but had a beautiful, giving nature. Unfortunately, the three sisters spent all of their time quarreling with one another. The parents had to continually stop the three sisters from fighting. Winter was coming, and the parents needed the help of the three girls in the garden if the family was to survive the winter cold and storms, but the three sisters could never stop their fighting long enough to be of use to anyone. The parents prayed for help, which came in an unexpected manner. The three sisters were transformed into plants, namely, corn, squash and beans. Henceforth, and for ever after, the three sisters would cooperate with one another and be a blessing to humankind. When planted together, corn, squash and beans, the "Three Sisters," form an ecosystem in which each plant helps the others to grow and thrive. The leaves of the squash provide shade, preventing moisture from evaporating and weeds from growing. Beans provide essential nitrogen for corn. The stalks of the corn give the beans a much-needed pole around which to climb.

Another, more fanciful story explained why there were so many tribes. Once, long ago, all humans and animals lived underground. One day, a brave mole climbed upward. He found a hole that took him to the surface, where he beheld light! What a beautiful world, filled with trees and rivers and the sky. The mole crawled back into the earth and told of the wonders he had seen. People began to climb upward and through the hole the mole had found. More and more people came pouring through the hole, until one fateful day when a fat chief got stuck in the hole. People pushed and pulled, but the chief was stuck for good. So not everyone made it to the surface.

The people who entered the new world walked on and on, exploring. They reached a wide river that blocked the way. But then a wondrous bird appeared and flapped its wings three times. The waters of the river parted, and the people walked across a path to the other side of the river. Many people crossed the river, but when the bird flew away, the waters came back. Some people did not get across.

The people who crossed the river continued on until they came to a high mountain. A deer led the people across the rocky mountain. But many people were left behind because an eagle chased away the friendly deer. Those who made it across the mountain next found themselves in a dense forest. The forest was so dense that people quickly got lost and could not find one another. Some went one way, and some went another way.

And so now you know why there are so many tribes living in so many different places.

Another tale tells of a curse associated with three large granite rocks that rise out of the waters of the Potomac River between Virginia and Washington, D.C., in an area once contested by the Powhatans and a neighboring tribe. Three young Powhatan warriors were taken prisoner by the rival tribe on the wrong side of the river and killed. Three young daughters of the local shaman were secretly in love with the Powhatan youths and vowed revenge. They planned to cross the river and beguile the warriors who had killed the youths they loved with their father's magic. They would then return to their side of the river and bring the murderers to Powhatan justice.

The sisters made a raft and launched out into the river, but as they tried to cross, a storm arose. The current was too fast and strong for them. The raft broke apart, and the sisters drowned, but before they did, they cursed the river and said that anyone who tried to cross at the spot where they went down would die. The storm raged all night and lightning struck the spot where the sisters had drowned. The next morning, all was calm on the river, but three large granite rocks had risen out of the water. To this day, those three boulders are known as the Three Sisters Rocks.

"HE WHOSE SOUL IS WHITE"

Jamestown, founded in 1607, was the first successful English settlement in North America. The settlement's only cash crop, tobacco, required constant expansion into the lands of the neighboring Powhatan Confederacy. Additionally, more and more Europeans kept arriving, all hungry for land. Tensions continued to grow between the Native population and the Europeans, until one war chief, Opechancanough, who was fiercely suspicious of and hostile to the English, led a coordinated series of surprise attacks that killed a quarter of the population of the English settlers in the Virginia colony.

Captain John Smith related in his *History of Virginia* that Powhatan warriors "came unarmed into our houses with deer, turkeys, fish, fruits, and other provisions to sell us." The warriors then grabbed any tools or weapons at hand and killed any settlers they found, including men, women and children.

But just who was this cunning and bloodthirsty Chief Opechancanough? Most people think that Captain John Smith was the first European to explore Virginia, but there is evidence that Spanish explorers beat Captain Smith by several decades. An attempt at colonization was made in 1570, when Governor Pedro Menendez of Florida authorized an expedition. At the time, it was believed that the Chesapeake was the long-sought short passage to China. Jesuit missionaries convinced the governor to send their small, unarmed expedition to the area as a forerunner to future colonization. On September 10, 1570, a small band of Jesuits headed by Father Segura, vice provincial of the Jesuits, settled near a place the Native Americans called Axacan.

The Jesuits were convinced that they could gain the trust of the Natives and willingly convert thousands to Christianity for one simple reason: they were accompanied by a prince of that country who had converted to Christianity. An earlier Spanish expedition had sailed into the Chesapeake Bay in 1560 and encountered Native Americans. A young son of one of the Powhatan chiefs either agreed to accompany the Spaniards or was made a captive when the Spaniards sailed away. The Spanish called the boy Paquiquino (little Francis). In September 1561, Paquiquino arrived in Spain, traveling to Seville, Cordoba and finally Madrid, where he was inspected by King Philip II. A year later, the boy arrived in Mexico City, where he became critically ill. Upon his recovery, Paquiquino was baptized Don Luís de Velasco in honor of his sponsor of the same name and subsequently received a Jesuit education. Don Luis returned to his own country with Father Segura and his Jesuit missionaries in 1570.

Shortly after returning, Don Luis rejected his Spanish name, renounced Christianity and returned to his people. In February 1571, he returned with a group of armed warriors and killed the eight Jesuit missionaries, sparing only a young boy named Alonzo who the Jesuit had brought as an altar boy. Alonzo eventually made his way to the village of a rival tribe and was finally rescued by a Spanish ship bringing supplies to the Jesuits.

When Governor Menendez learned of the massacre, he sailed for Axacan. In early 1572, the Spanish returned to Virginia, capturing and hanging a number of Powhatan men accused of participating in the massacre. The backsliding former convert Don Luis was never located. Some historians believe that he was later to give the English settlers at Jamestown trouble, speculating that Don Luis was in fact Opechancanough, the Powhatan chief who organized the ferocious massacre of English settlers in 1622. The name Opechancanough means "He Whose Soul Is White" in the language used by the Powhatan people.

The Virginia colonists survived the attacks, barely, and retaliated in kind, killing and burning. An uneasy peace was finally established, but tensions continued to be high until April 18, 1644, when Chief Opechancanough, said to have been in his nineties, had another go at wiping out the colony. This new war raged for two years until Opechancanough was captured by the royal governor, William Berkeley. The captured chief was paraded through Jamestown, taunted by a jeering mob. Opechancanough lamented, "If it had been my fortune to take Sir William Berkeley prisoner, I would not have meanly exposed him as a show to my people." The chief died shortly thereafter, shot in the back while trying to escape.

While some historians believe that Opechancanough may have been the Powhatan boy known as Don Luis and educated by the Spanish, others suggest that Opechancanough was a nephew or cousin of Don Luis. We may never know the truth, but we do know that Opechancanough was a fierce and charismatic warrior with an implacable grudge against Europeans.

COLONIAL TIMES

WILD PONIES

A Spanish galleon on its way to Peru was blown northward toward the Virginia capes in the sixteenth century. We can imagine its fate on that last stormy night as it struck the top of a reef, or maybe just rolled over it, caught athwartship by a breaker. As soon as the Spanish realized that they were about to go on the rocks, they dropped anchor. It was near midnight. The pilot was standing on the deck holding his astrolabe at the ready, waiting for a break in the clouds to take a sighting on a star. As the ship rolled, his astrolabe slipped into the sea.

The vessel had begun to turn around on itself, but the next moment, it was broken apart. From its gaping hull spilled cannonballs and lead ingots, along with the kitchen equipment. Men and horses came tumbling out of it—scattered, thrown onto the beach or carried out to sea by the tide. The aftercastle broke away from the shattered hull and drifted eastward. The captain's cabin emptied out its treasures and its passengers, sprinkling the seabed with a thousand ephemeral things. Were there survivors? We can't be sure about the sailors, but we do know that horses survived. They were the ancestors of today's famous "wild ponies of Chincoteague," domesticated horses that reverted to a wild state. These hardy survivors endured heat, mosquitos, stormy weather and scant food on a barren barrier island.

That island was not actually Chincoteague but nearby Assateague Island. Chincoteague is the gateway to the Virginia portion of Assateague Island (shared with Maryland) and the Chincoteague National Wildlife Refuge. The famous wild horses are now split into two main herds, one on the Virginia side and one on the Maryland side of Assateague (separated by a fence). Assateague Bay separates Assateague Island from Chincoteague Island.

Chincoteague ponies have short legs, thick manes and large, round bellies. The ponies primarily eat the saltwater cord grass that grows in the marshes on Assateague Island. They must eat almost constantly to get enough nutrition from this sparse diet. The wild ponies have divided themselves into bands of from 2 to 12 animals, with each band occupying a home range. Each band has 1 dominant stallion, with the rest of the band consisting of mares with whom the stallion breeds. The Chincoteague Volunteer Fire Company, which owns and manages the Virginia herd, maintains the herd size at 150 adult ponies; 70 new foals are born every spring on the Virginia side of the island.

When Twentieth Century Fox produced the movie *Misty of Chincoteague* in 1961, based on Marguerite Henry's best-selling children's book, Chincoteague Island became famous. The tiny village became a major tourist destination. Henry's book tells the story of two children who live with their grandparents on Chincoteague Island. The children long to own a wild Chincoteague pony mare named Phantom that has eluded sale by escaping the roundup men on the annual Pony Penning Day for the last two years. At the next Pony Penning Day, one of the children captures Phantom because she has been slowed down looking out for her new foal, Misty. At the horse auction following the roundup, a man from the mainland buys Phantom and Misty for his son before the children can bid. In the end, the children are able to buy Phantom and Misty. Phantom is tamed, and the children race her on the next Pony Penning Day. Phantom wins the race but longs for freedom when she sees the wild herd she once belonged to being released to swim back to Assateague Island. The children release Phantom. She gallops to join the herd. Misty remains with the children.

Marguerite Henry's book acquainted the world with the traditional Chincoteague festival called "Pony Penning." On the last Wednesday in July, the Virginia herd of horses is rounded up. The herd then swims from Assateague Island to nearby Chincoteague Island. A horse auction is held the following day, where most of the foals are sold off in order to prevent overpopulation of the herd. The proceeds from the sales go to support the Chincoteague Volunteer Fire Department.

For the "Pony Swim," the so-called saltwater cowboys round up the wild ponies living on Assateague Island. The saltwater cowboys, who care for the ponies throughout the year, are members of the Chincoteague Volunteer

Fire Department, many of whom have held the position for decades. It is considered a great honor to be selected as a saltwater cowboy. The actual Pony Swim happens between 7:00 a.m. and 2:00 p.m., depending on slack tide. The swim lasts for about ten minutes. The saltwater cowboys ride horses across the channel and assist any ponies, especially foals, that may have a hard time crossing. The first foal to reach the shore is named king or queen of the festival.

Pony penning was practiced as early as the 1700s. Unclaimed animals were branded or marked for ownership at an annual event that also involved eating, drinking and revelry. The earliest known description of Pony Penning was published in 1835. The penning continued on both Assateague and Chincoteague Islands for years. By 1885, they were held on Assateague one day and Chincoteague the next. In 1909, the last Wednesday and Thursday of July were set as the official dates for the yearly events. By the 1920s, Chincoteague Island had become a regional tourist attraction. In 1922, a causeway was built between the island and the Virginia mainland. After fire ravaged the village of Chincoteague, the Volunteer Fire Company was established. In 1924, the first official Pony Penning Day was held. Foals were auctioned to raise money for fire equipment. Pony Penning Day has been held annually ever since.

PIRATE TREASURES

Are there buried pirate treasures? Although most pirates spent their money as quickly as they stole it, there were often occasions when pirates buried their valuables before going into battle. If captured, few pirates wanted to be caught with incriminating evidence. Most pirates died suddenly and unexpectedly. Many were killed in battle. Hundreds drowned. Many died of disease. No matter what the reason for burying the treasure, it is safe to say that great fortunes were buried on lonely beaches by roving pirates who never returned.

Along the coast of North America, the two areas most favored by pirates were the waters of Charleston, South Carolina, and off Virginia's Chesapeake capes. The capes were popular because most of the shipping from Virginia and Maryland was funneled into the Atlantic through the narrow mouth of the Chesapeake Bay, between Cape Charles and Cape Henry.

For well over a century, Virginia became a haven for pirates and an object for plunder. The first recorded instance of piracy in Virginia occurred in 1610. Throughout the seventeenth century, there were scattered incidents of piracy. In 1660, for instance, when England was at war with the Dutch, Governor William Berkeley complained that the "seas are so full of pirates that it is almost impossible for any ships to go home in safety." And by 1678, Algerian pirates plundered so many ships off the Virginia coast that the local merchants and planters began to demand convoy service for ships that carried their goods.

By the 1680s, the pirates began to make inland excursions to plunder and terrorize plantation families. Unknown numbers of pirate ships made a haven of the shadowed inlets and small islands in the area of Chesapeake Bay, where the crews provisioned their vessels at leisure. In 1682, a pirate ship landed at the mouth of the York River and its crew sacked two plantation homes, taking silver plate and cash as well as food. Until then, the colonists had traded with the pirates; but in 1684, a proclamation prohibited "the King's subjects from trading, harboring or corresponding with pirates."

Despite the king's proclamation, many wealthy colonists formed syndicates to fit out pirate vessels, sharing the plunder with the crews. At first, these ships were sent to prey on Spanish shipping in the West Indies, but toward the end of the seventeenth century, they discovered a more profitable and less hazardous area in which to operate: the Red Sea, where Captain William Kidd became the most notorious pirate of all time.

During the summer of 1699, matters reached a critical stage along the coasts of Maryland, Virginia and the Carolinas. There were too many pirates operating off the Atlantic shore to provide booty for all. No longer content with glamorous plunder of jewels and precious metals, they seized every cargo for which there was a market, even such commonplace products as tobacco. Pirates became attracted to any concentration of wealth when those who held the wealth were too weak to defend it.

Virginians began posting pirate lookouts. Constant patrols were set up on both land and sea to detect pirates before they could enter the colony. In March 1699, the captain of HMS *Essex Prize* was ordered to apprehend pirates and "most especially to look after Kidd, the Pirate." Several months later, one of Kidd's ships was reported near the Delaware coast, waiting to unload a quantity of silver plate and gold. About the same time, a native of Accomack County wrote Governor Nicholson that a forty-two-gun ship belonging to the notorious Captain Kidd, together with an eighteen-gun sloop, was off the Virginia coast.

For a while, it appeared that Virginia might become a refuge for pirates who had sailed with William Kidd. Sixty men who had deserted Kidd in Madagascar were reported to be coming to Virginia to settle down. Other of Kidd's men who had escaped from prison were also bound for the colony. Kidd veered northward from Virginia, where he was captured. He was transported to England and hanged in 1701 for murder and piracy. Captain Kidd did not, however, leave Virginia without first leaving a touch of his legend. Many people believe that one of Kidd's treasures was buried on Hog Island, Northampton County.

Between 1702 and 1713, the Queen Anne's War raged off the Virginia capes, and pirates became privateers in the honorable service of their respective nations. Most pirates migrated to the West Indies, where the spoils were richer during this period.

By 1716, the vultures of the sea were beginning to return to Virginia from the Caribbean in increasing numbers. So great had the pirate threat grown that no vessel dared sail through the Virginia capes unless convoyed by a man-of-war. In 1718, a royal pardon was granted to all pirates who would surrender themselves and renounce piracy. Two well-equipped royal frigates, HMS *Lyme* and HMS *Pearl*, were dispatched to enforce royal justice.

The only real menace left after the issuance of the royal pardon and the arrival of the Royal Navy was Captain Edward Teach, known to history as Blackbeard.

These were the pirates of Virginia's history: blood-drenched rascals who, besides tales of adventure, left future generations a few great chests bound with iron. These chests, filled with the gold and jewels of countless ocean raids, lie buried along the coasts of Virginia, waiting for a storm or a lucky accident to uncover them after a sleep of centuries. Search if you will for the Chincoteague Cache, which was described in a letter sent to one George Wilson in 1750:

> *There are three creeks lying 100 paces or more north of the second inlet above Chincoteague Island, Virginia, which is at the southward end of the peninsula. At the head of the third creek to the northward is a bluff facing the Atlantic Ocean with three cedar trees growing on it, each about 1.5 yards apart. Between the trees I buried ten iron bound chests, bars of silver, gold, diamonds and jewels to the sum of 200,000 pounds sterling. Go to the woody knoll secretly and remove the treasure.*

This letter resides in the British Naval Records Office. Charles Wilson, who wrote the letter, was in jail, awaiting hanging (which fate he eventually met) for the crime of piracy on the high seas. Prison authorities intercepted the letter, so it never reached his brother. The treasure remains undiscovered.

Alternatively, one could search for Blackbeard's gold. Clement Downing, an officer aboard HMS *Salisbury*, wrote this account in 1737 (see *A Compendious History of the Indian Wars; with an Account of the Rise, Progress, Strength and Forces of Angria the Pyrate, etc.*):

At Guzarat I met with a Portugese named Anthony de Sylvestre; he came down with two other Portugese and two Dutchmen to take on in the Moor's service, as many Europeans do. This Anthony told me he had been among the pirates, and that he had belonged to one of the sloops in Virginia when Blackbeard was taken. He informed me that if it should be my lot ever to go to York River…near an island called Mulberry Island, provided we went on shore at the watering place where the shipping used most commonly to ride, that there the pirates had buried considerable sums of money in great chests well clamped with iron plates. As to my part, I never was that way, nor much acquainted with any that ever used those parts; but I have made inquiry, and am informed that there is such a place as Mulberry Island. If any person who uses those parts should think it worthwhile to dig a little way at the upper end of a small cove, where it is convenient to the land, he would soon find whether the information I have was well grounded. Fronting the land place are five trees, among which, he said, the money was hid. I cannot warrant the truth of this account; but if I were ever to go there, I should find some means or other to satisfy myself, as it could not be a great deal out of my way. If anybody should obtain benefit of this, if it pleases God they were to come to England, 'tis hoped they will remember whence they had the information.

It is safe to say that Downing never made use of his secret information, as he died penniless in England. Of his treasure, Blackbeard himself said, "The devil knows where I've hid my money and I know where I've hid it; and the longest liver of the twain will get it all."

GENERAL BRADDOCK'S
LOST TREASURE

One of Virginia's must intriguing legends involves buried treasure, specifically the lost treasure of British general Edward Braddock. The Seven Years' War was fought across several continents and the world's oceans between the British and French, together with their European allies. In North America, the English colonies were locked in mortal combat with their age-old enemy the French and their Indian allies. In February 1755, General Edward Braddock landed at the port of Alexandria, Virginia, with one thousand British regulars. Braddock's expedition was just one part of a massive British offensive against the French in North America that summer. His mission was to drive the French out of Fort Duquesne (now Pittsburgh) and destroy French resistance along the frontier.

Some provincials—including Benjamin Franklin, who was helping to provision the army—cautioned the general about over-reliance on traditional European military methods in the American wilderness. Franklin told the general:

> The only danger I apprehend of obstruction to your march, is from Ambuscades of Indians, who by constant practice are dexterous in laying and executing them. And the slender line near four miles long, which your army must make, may expose it to be attacked by surprise in its flanks, and to be cut like a thin thread into several pieces which, from their distance cannot come up in time to support each other.

General Edward Braddock led his army to destruction in 1755.

According to Franklin, "He [Braddock] smiled at my ignorance, and replied, 'These savages may, indeed, be a formidable enemy to your raw American militia, but upon the King's regular and disciplined troops, sir, it is impossible they should make any impression.'"

Braddock's troubles started almost immediately. He could never get used to the terrain and distances in America. The Potomac River, which on a map looked like a highway far to the west, was made unnavigable by rocks and falls just a few miles above Alexandria. The expedition faced an enormous logistical challenge: moving a large body of men, equipment and heavy artillery across densely wooded and mountainous terrain 110 miles into western Pennsylvania. Heavy rains from April to June made the land between Alexandria and the fur trading town of Winchester a sea of mud. The expedition progressed slowly because Braddock insisted in building a road to Fort Duquesne. In some cases, the column moved as few as two miles a day.

Arriving at the village of Newgate (renamed Centreville in 1798), only twenty-seven miles from Alexandria, the cannons and wagons became hopelessly mired in mud and clay. In an act of desperation, Braddock ordered some of the artillery buried. Taking aside a small group of soldiers, he buried two of the brass cannons after pouring the gold coins used to pay the troops into the open ends of the barrels. The mouths of the cannons were then sealed with wooden plugs.

The general carefully noted the location of the treasure, "fifty paces east of a spring where the road runs north and south." The road of which he spoke is now called Braddock Road, where the road runs north to intersect U.S. Route 29-211 in Centreville, Virginia.

Braddock marched on to disaster in western Pennsylvania. Ambushed in the thick forests, the red-coated British were easy targets for the concealed French and Indians. The few trusted officers who knew the secret of the buried treasure were killed in battle. Finally, with General Braddock mortally wounded, the army managed to retreat. Braddock died on the night of July 13, 1755. His last words were, "Who would have thought it?"

General Braddock's papers were sent to England. Years later, an archivist found the account of the buried gold located in Virginia. A special committee was dispatched to search for the gold but returned to England empty-handed. So, to this day, two brass cannons, filled with gold, lie beneath the soil of Virginia.

So here you have the legend of Braddock's gold. But where did it come from, and how true is it? In 1982, Douglas Phillips and Barnaby Nygren wrote a monograph titled *An Inquiry into the Validity of the Legend of Braddock's Gold in Northern Virginia.* Phillips and Nygren assert that they were unable to find any reference to General Braddock's treasure dating before 1954, when the article "A Buried Treasure" by Charles J. Gilliss appeared in the 1954 yearbook of the Historical Society of Fairfax County. The popular media was quick to take up the Gilliss article, and numerous newspaper articles and book chapters have flowed from this original source. Problematically, the Gilliss article cited no references. The historical society's commentary on the Gilliss article at the time of its publication was, "Mr. Gilliss is a lifelong resident of Prince William County. Legends such as this are a most delightful part of our history."

When Phillips and Nygren compared historical documents to the Gilliss account, red flags went up. The Gilliss account, in many of its details, was not borne out by Braddock's own orderly book or accounts of the time by his officers. The army seems to have made good marching time and encountered no inclement weather. In short, there is no evidence to suggest that any difficulties were encountered where the legend suggests the gold is buried. Phillips and Nygren next mapped out Braddock's line of march, based on documents of the time, demonstrating that the column came nowhere near Centreville. "All the firsthand accounts, based on diaries, orderly books, letters, maps, and court records…show that not only are certain elements of the legend probably false, but also that Braddock's troops took a march route which never brought them within ten miles of Centreville."

Phillips and Nygren conclude, "While it is obvious to the authors that the probability of Braddock's Gold being buried in Fairfax County is virtually nil, the possibility, small as it may be, of gold being buried elsewhere along Braddock's route does exist, and in that may be the source of the Northern Virginia legend."

Which brings us to an interesting treasure legend from North Huntingdon Township in western Pennsylvania (as recorded on its website):

> *During the time of his expedition into the North Huntingdon area, General Edward Braddock camped one evening with his army near what is now*

known as Circleville....Braddock requested that the men wait until after the battle to get paid because a number of them would be killed. Therefore, he reasoned there would be fewer to divide the gold. The men voted in favor of Braddock's plan. Braddock then suggested they hide the gold instead of taking it into battle, lest it fall into the hands of the French and Indians.

And so the legend lives on another day.

COLONEL CHISWELL, THE CELEBRITY MURDERER

When we think of the Virginia of colonial times, the Virginia of Washington, Madison and Jefferson, we seldom think of the word *murder*. And yet behind the façade of graceful mansions and quaint cobblestone streets, evil lurked. Take, for example, the strange case of Colonel John Chiswell, someone today we might call "a celebrity murderer."

Colonel John Chiswell was a very busy and important man. He owned a huge plantation, he was a member of the House of Burgesses and he was a colonel in the militia. His wife was from a fine old family. The royal governor, Francis Fauquier, was a close friend. His son-in-law was treasurer of the colony. This was not a little man unknown in the colony. Soon he would be even better known.

On June 3, 1766, Colonel Chiswell attended a session of the Cumberland County Court to look after some land deals. That evening, he entered Benjamin Mosby's tavern. One Robert Routlidge, a blunt Scottish merchant who had had dealings with Chiswell before, approached the colonel. Routlidge was clearly drunk—and not just a little drunk. Routlidge proceeded to insult Chiswell and then threw a glass of wine in his face. The short-fused Chiswell picked up a pair of fire tongs and made for Routlidge. The crowd in the room restrained him. He next came at Routlidge with a candlestick. Again, he was restrained. Next, he picked up a punchbowl and made to break it over Routlidge's head. Again, he was restrained. A sheriff entered and ordered Colonel Chiswell to leave, which he did, only to return moments later carrying a sword.

The sheriff tried to keep him from Routlidge, but Chiswell bellowed that he would "run through any man" who tried to stop him. Routlidge and Chiswell exchanged curses across the room until finally Chiswell called Routlidge a "Presbyterian fellow," which was too much for Routlidge, who broke free from those trying to calm him and squarely faced Chiswell. In the next instant, the colonel ran his sword directly into Routlidge's heart. The merchant fell dead. Colonel Chiswell handed the sword to a servant for cleaning and then ordered a bowl of punch, declaring, "He deserves his fate, damn him. I aimed at his heart and I have hit it." The gaping sheriff immediately took Chiswell into custody.

The cold-blooded murder of an unarmed man in front of a room full of witnesses, including a sheriff—was this an open-and-shut case? Not according to Colonel Chiswell's attorney. According to the defense, due to his drunkenness, Routlidge threw himself on the colonel's sword. The incident was a mere accident. After hearing the testimony of the witnesses, the examining court found sufficient evidence to prosecute the case. Chiswell was held without bail, and an under-sheriff was ordered to transport the colonel to Williamsburg, where he was to be jailed in chains while awaiting trial before the governor. News of the murder spread fast among Virginia's power elite. Three of the governor's closest confidants intercepted the under-sheriff and his prisoner before they could reach Williamsburg. The distinguished deputation ordered the under-sheriff to release Chiswell on bail. The colonel returned to the comforts of his townhouse in Williamsburg, where he remained in seclusion.

Was the whole matter to be swept under the rug by Chiswell's powerful friends? Perhaps it could have been and would have been had it not been for one Robert Bolling, who published an anonymous query in the *Virginia Gazette* of June 20, 1766. Bolling broke the story to the general public:

> *Upon an inquisition taken before the Coroner in Cumberland county, Robert Routlidge was found to be murdered (June 3d) by a sword in the hand of John Chiswell, Esq; whereupon he was committed to the county prison, and the examining Court, upon full evidence (refusing to bail him on a motion for that purpose) ordered him to the public prison, as the law directs, to be tried for murder.*

Bolling continued the anonymous query by relating the special treatment given to Colonel Chiswell by the judges of the general court: "But before he was delivered to the keeper of the public prison, the Judges of the General

Colonel John Chiswell was on his way to trial in Williamsburg when freed by powerful friends.

Court, out of sessions, took him from the sheriff who conveyed him from Cumberland, and admitted him to bail, without seeing the record of his examination in the county, or examining any of the witnesses against him."

Bolling's query came to a thunderous summation:

> *I ask, whether this act of the three Judges of the General Court be legal. If it is legal, I have nothing more to say. If it is not legal, then I ask whether the act of these Judges has not a tendency to overturn the laws and constitution of the country, by their exercising an extra judicial power and controlling the course of law in a case of the highest consequence to the safety of the* [king's] *subject*[s]*? Whether the bail taken by these Judges in an extra judicial manner can be liable on their recognizance, if Mr. Chiswell should not appear to take his trial? If they are not liable, whether it is not in fact a rescue, under pretense of law, of a person charged with an atrocious crime?*

As the facts became known, outrage spread among the general public. Increasingly angry voices were raised about both the murder and the special privileges that were being granted Colonel John Chiswell. The murder was fast becoming "the crime of the century," pitting the power elite against the common man in a contest over equality before the law.

In fact, Colonel Chiswell never came to trial. Either pressured by friends or collapsing under the nervous strain, Colonel Chiswell committed suicide in his Williamsburg townhouse. The *Virginia Gazette* reported that he died of "nervous fits, owing to a constant uneasiness of mind." This did not entirely end the matter. By now, the people so distrusted their political masters that they suspected a plot to smuggle a still very much alive John Chiswell out of the colony. An angry mob stopped Chiswell's funeral procession and demanded to see the body. The coffin was duly opened and Colonel Chiswell's body publicly identified.

THE COURTSHIP
OF MARTHA WASHINGTON

Conduct manuals appearing in the late eighteenth century advised the young women of Virginia to steer a middle course between undue familiarity, which was dangerous, and cold reserve, which made them undesirable. Smoothly engineered marriages among the wealthy required that children recognize suitable marriage partners, weeding out frauds, rakes and gold diggers. The successful transmission from parent to child of standards of quality, breeding and social position prevented children of the elite from straying too far from people of whom their parents approved. Marriageable age in Virginia was considered to begin at fourteen for women and the early twenties for men.

Well-to-do families saw to it that their daughters acquired an education that included practical, literary and ornamental skills. These included cooking, sewing and household management; reading, writing and perhaps a little arithmetic and French; and a number of other niceties such as polished manners, musical training, dancing, drawing and fancy needlework.

Courting took place at organized functions such as dances, horse races and church. Dancing was an important courting ritual among the wealthy. It was considered a good way to determine a potential marriage partner's physical soundness, as well as the state of their teeth and breath. Dancing taught poise, grace and balance, especially important to women who had to learn to remain in their "compass," or the area of movement allowed by their clothing. Balls often lasted three to four days and took all day and most of the night. They were the primary means of socializing in Virginia.

Martha was slightly younger than the average Virginia bride, who married at age twenty-two.

Women, then as now, had ways of making themselves more alluring. Among the elite, cosmetics were commonly worn. Almost everyone had a pock-marked face due to the widespread scourge of smallpox, but a handsomely pocked face was not considered unattractive, only an excessively pocked one. Flour, white lead, orrisroot and cornstarch were common bases to produce the esthetic of a pure white face. Over these, red rouge was used to highlight cheekbones in a manner that would be considered exaggerated by modern standards but was most effective in the dim light afforded by candles in the eighteenth century. Lip color and rouge were made from crushed cochineal beetles. Cochineal was an expensive imported commodity; country women substituted berry stains. Carbon was used to highlight eyebrows and lashes, which were groomed with fine combs. The key aspects of the eighteenth-century cosmetic look were a complexion somewhere between white and pale, red cheeks and red lips. The ideal woman had a high forehead; plump, rosy cheeks; pale skin; and small lips, soft and red, with the lower lip being slightly larger, thus creating a rosebud effect. Although bathing one's entire body was not a regular occurrence in the eighteenth century, the daily washing of one's face and hands was the norm in elite social circles.

An almanac essay titled "Love and Acquaintance with the Fair Sex" assures us that men were incapable of "resistance" against a woman's "attractive charms of an enchanting outside in the sprightly bloom of happy nature; against the graces of wit and politeness; against the lure of modesty and sweetness." Of course, some men felt uneasy about female allurements, which could account for the introduction of a bill before the British Parliament in 1770 titled "An Act to Protect Men from Being Beguiled into Marriage by False Adornments." The proposed act read:

> *All women, of whatever rank, age, profession or degree, whether virgins, maids or widows, that shall, from and after such Act, impose upon, seduce or betray into matrimony, any of His Majesty's subjects, by the use of scents, paints, cosmetic washes, artificial teeth, false hair, Spanish wool, iron stays, hoops, high-heeled shoes and bolstered hips, shall incur the penalty of the law in force against witchcraft and like misdemeanours and that the marriage upon conviction shall stand null and void.*

To the everlasting regret of some, the act did not become law.

The ideal woman, according to "Advice to Unmarried Ladies," appearing in the *American Herald* in 1789, was demure, modest and avoided confrontation in conversation. Physical traits included "a pretty foot, good teeth, pretty hands and arms, and the finest voice."

In upper- and middle-class families, a successful courtship concluded with the two fathers working out financial arrangements. These arrangements differed greatly depending on the wealth and position of the parents, but generally, the young man's parents were expected to be the most generous, providing land, a house, cattle and tools. The bride's parents contributed clothing, furniture, linens and money. When all financial arrangements were settled, the banns were read in church, and the couple was officially considered to be engaged.

At the age of eighteen, Martha Dandridge stood about five feet tall, somewhat shorter than the average five feet, three inches of women of the day. By all accounts, she was lovely with a lively personality, warm, dutiful, strong and sincere. She received the education typical of girls of her class. She met her first husband, Daniel Parke Custis, at their local Anglican church. Custis was the son of one of the wealthiest men in Virginia, John Custis IV, who owned thousands of acres of land, had almost three hundred slaves and sat on the Governor's Council in Williamsburg. Daniel Parke Custis was some twenty years older than Martha Dandridge. He lived on his own plantation, White House, situated four miles downstream from the Dandridge home on the Pamunkey River. When word of his son's interest in Martha surfaced, John Custis IV initially opposed the match. He insisted that the Dandridge family lacked sufficient wealth and status to marry into his family and threatened to disinherit his son. Although Martha's father owned five hundred acres of land and fifteen to twenty slaves, he was not close to being among the wealthiest men in Virginia.

When Daniel pursued the match over his father's objections, family friends intervened with his father on their behalf. Martha arranged a meeting with Daniel's father where she made her own case. The elder Custis concluded that Martha was "beautiful and sweet tempered" and gave his consent for the marriage. Martha Dandridge and Daniel Parke Custis married on May 15, 1750. Almost nineteen years old, Martha was slightly younger than the average Virginia bride, who married at age twenty-two. At thirty-eight, Daniel Parke Custis was nearly twenty years older than his new wife and significantly older than the average Virginia man, who married for the first time at age twenty-seven. The marriage lasted seven years. Martha then found herself a widow and one of the wealthiest women in the colonies.

Martha did not remain a widow long as suitors began to appear at her plantation, including Colonel of Virginia Militia George Washington, a celebrated hero of the recent war with the French and Indians. Washington sprang from the moderately prosperous Virginia gentry rather than one of the leading planter families. His background mirrored Martha's own. In March 1758, George visited Martha twice; the second time, he came away greatly encouraged.

In addition to all of the natural beauty that entails to a woman of great fortune, after seven years of marriage, Martha was still physically desirable. Charles Carter, a Virginia planter of far greater wealth and status than Colonel Washington, wrote to his brother about what a beauty she was and how he hoped to "arouse a flame in her breast." Carter failed, and Martha Dandridge Custis married George Washington on January 6, 1759. The couple honeymooned for several weeks before setting up housekeeping at Washington's Mount Vernon estate.

FROM THE AMERICAN REVOLUTION TO THE WAR OF 1812

GEORGE WASHINGTON: LEGENDS AND LORE

Mason Locke Weems (1759–1825), known to history as Parson Weems, wrote *The Life of Washington* in 1800. Weems's book served as the jumping-off place for many fanciful stories about the life of George Washington, none more famous than the legend of George Washington and the cherry tree. In this story, six-year-old George Washington, excited about receiving a new hatchet, gets carried away and cuts down his father's prized young cherry tree. When George's father demands to know what happened to the tree, young George, "looking at his father with the sweet face of youth brightened with the inexpressible charm of all-conquering truth," confesses that he did the deed. "I cannot tell a lie," says George. George's father is overwhelmed by the young boy's virtue and honesty, and all is forgiven.

Weems wrote the biography to amplify his subject. His subject was "Washington, the hero, and the demigod." It has been said of his writing, "If the tales aren't true, they should be. They are too pretty to be classified with the myths." Sometimes it is hard to think of George Washington as a man because of what Parson Weems and other earlier biographers wrote. A marble statue—yes. The guy on the dollar bill—yes. But a man? So let's consider his aches and pains to bring him down to earth—specifically his painful teeth.

Despite his best efforts to care for his teeth, Washington lost his first tooth at the age of twenty-four. Almost every year thereafter, Washington suffered from severe toothaches, followed by the painful extraction of the teeth.

PUBLISHED BY CURRIER & IVES   Copyright 1876 by Currier & Ives, N.Y.   125 NASSAU ST. NEW YORK

THE SPIRIT OF THE UNION.

Lo! on high the glorious form,
Of Washington lights all the gloom.
And words of warning seem to come
From out the portal of his tomb;

Americans your Fathers shed
Their blood to rear the Union's fane,
Then let your blood as free be given,
The bond of Union to maintain.

Many fanciful stories have been written about the life of George Washington; the truth is even stranger.

Washington's teeth continued to deteriorate, making it hard for him to chew without pain. In 1773, at the age of forty-one, Washington wrote to a London merchant thanking him for his gift of two large stone jars of pickled tripe, which is soft and easy to eat.

By the age of forty-nine, Washington was wearing false teeth wired to his remaining ones. By the time he was fifty-seven and being sworn in for the first time as president of the United States, Washington had one remaining real tooth. That year, he received the first of four full sets of dentures made by John Greenwood, fashioned from hippopotamus ivory and human teeth.

Washington owned eight sets of dentures during his lifetime. None of these was made of wood, as some legends suggest, but all were uncomfortable and painful to use. The dentures distorted the look of Washington's mouth and inhibited him from smiling.

Other Washington artifacts lend themselves to Virginia lore. Take, for example, two historically priceless documents, the wills of George and Martha Washington, now housed in the Fairfax County Courthouse in Fairfax, Virginia.

During the Civil War, Federal troops occupied the Fairfax area. The clerk of court instructed his wife to take George Washington's will to the home of their daughter near Warrenton, Virginia. The will was placed in a chest that also contained family silver. The chest was buried in the wine cellar and covered with coal. In 1862, the will was taken to Richmond for safekeeping. The will was folded when it was moved to Richmond. As a result, the brittle pages were damaged, and every page was broken. In an attempt to prevent further breakage, some of the broken pages were sewn together with needle and thread. In 1865, the will was returned to the Fairfax County Courthouse. In 1910, William Berwick restored George Washington's will using a conservation process called crêpeline lamination. This technique involved coating each page of the will with a paste of wheat starch and water and then embedding a fine silk net into the paste.

During the Civil War, Martha Washington's will remained at the Fairfax County Courthouse. In 1862, the courthouse was vandalized by Union troops, and Martha Washington's will was stolen by Brevet Brigadier General David Thomson, who, shortly before his death, gave the will to his daughter Mary Thomson. Miss Thomson sold the will to Wall Street financier and avid art collector J. Pierpont Morgan. The Commonwealth of Virginia pursued the will's return all the way to the Supreme Court of the United States of America. In 1915, prior to the Supreme Court hearing the case, Morgan's son returned the stolen will to the Commonwealth of Virginia.

And then there is the story of the Civil War odyssey of Washington's silver.

George Washington Parke Custis and his sister Nelly were raised at Mount Vernon by George and Martha Washington. When Martha Washington died in 1802, her will bequeathed "all the silver plate of every kind of which I shall die possessed, together with the two large plated cooler the four small plated coolers with the bottle castors," to her grandson George Washington Parke Custis.

Custis died in 1857, and the silver passed to his daughter Mary, the wife of Robert E. Lee. Mary and Robert E. Lee lived in Arlington House until 1861, when Virginia seceded from the Union and Lee went south to join the Confederate army. The Washington silver was packed into trunks and sent to Richmond. Lee then sent the trunks on to the Virginia Military Institute (VMI) in Lexington, Virginia, for safekeeping.

There the silver remained safe until June 1864, when Union general David Hunter raided the Valley of Virginia and advanced on Lexington. The Washington silver was saved from destruction by the actions of the VMI superintendent Francis Smith and ordnance sergeant John Hampsey. As Federal troops advanced on Lexington, Smith ordered Hampsey to bury the two large trunks that held the Washington silver. As the buildings on the VMI campus burned, the Washington silver lay safely hidden beneath the ground.

After the war, Robert E. Lee became the president of Washington College in Lexington (later Washington and Lee University). In the fall of 1865, as the Lees settled into their new home, they called upon their "trusty friend" John Hampsey to help unearth the two large chests of buried treasure. Hampsey escorted Robert E. Lee Jr. to the burial site, and the general's son later reminisced, "I was sent out with him to dig it up and bring it in. We found it safe and sound, but black with mould and damp."

The Washington silver remained in the Lees' home at Washington College until Mary's death in 1873, after which the silver was bequeathed to all branches of the family. Some of the descendants have donated pieces to the Mount Vernon Ladies' Association, the custodians of George Washington's Mount Vernon estate.

DID GEORGE WASHINGTON HAVE A SON?

D id George Washington have one or more illegitimate sons? We know from traditional history that George and Martha Washington were married on January 6, 1759. Both were in their late twenties. Martha, a widow, had already borne four children. The marriage lasted forty happy years, without issue, until the general's death in 1799. Some have speculated that Washington was sterile. Others have suggested that Martha could no longer have children stemming from complications from her last pregnancy. We know Martha did not give George a son. But did another woman?

Venus was a slave who belonged to John Augustine, George Washington's brother, who lived in Westmoreland County, some ninety-five miles from Mount Vernon. Linda Allen Bryant, a direct descendant of a slave named West Ford (1784?–1863), points to correspondence between George and his brother John to argue that George visited his brother's plantation in 1784 and that a gap in Washington's personal diary that year could account for a sexual liaison during this visit. According to an oral tradition passed down in the Ford family, a story first publicized in the 1940s, when confronted by her mistress, Hannah Washington, the pregnant Venus confessed the paternity of her child: "The old General be the father, Mistress." Bryant makes her case in a book titled *I Cannot Tell a Lie: The True Story of George Washington's African American Descendants*.

There is definitely evidence to support the fact that West Ford, his mother, Venus, and other members of his family received preferential treatment. This favored treatment, however, was given not by George and Martha Washington but by the family of John Augustine. West Ford moved to Mount Vernon in 1802, three years after George Washington died. In his will, George Washington left the Mount Vernon estate to Bushrod Washington (1762–1829), his nephew. Bushrod (later a justice of the Supreme Court) moved to Mount Vernon and brought West Ford with him. West Ford was freed at the age of twenty-one. A freedman, West Ford was employed by Bushrod Washington as an overseer at Mount Vernon for the next twenty-three years until Bushrod's death in 1829. Ford continued to work for the Washington family after Bushrod's death, even though he had inherited 119 acres of land on nearby Hunting Creek from Bushrod. In 1833, West Ford sold this land and purchased 214 acres adjacent to it. Today, the area is known as Gum Springs. Gum Springs has some 2,500 residents, and as many as 500 are descendants of the slave families who served at Mount Vernon. After working on the Mount Vernon estate for almost sixty years, West Ford had become a well-known individual in the Mount Vernon/Alexandria area and throughout the country. He had also become the second-wealthiest free Black person in Fairfax County. He was not only well known but also held a prominent place in the local community, respected by whites and Blacks alike.

Based primarily on the family's oral tradition, the descendants of West Ford continue to insist that George Washington is part of the family tree. At an earlier time, this claim might have been dismissed out of hand, but the case of Thomas Jefferson and Sally Hemmings requires that all of the evidence be reviewed critically and in depth. A similar scenario existed with Hemmings, a slave owned by Thomas Jefferson. Her descendants claimed that Jefferson fathered one or more of Hemmings's children. Critics scoffed. But DNA analysis compared the Y-chromosome DNA from the living male-line descendants of Jefferson and Hemmings, and in 1998, the British science journal *Nature* published the results of the DNA study linking a member of the Jefferson family to Hemmings. The Thomas Jefferson Memorial Foundation, the custodians of Monticello, then issued a report in January 2000 concluding that Thomas Jefferson was the father of at least one and perhaps all the children of Sally Hemmings. The descendants of West Ford are attempting to conduct a similar DNA analysis to prove or disprove the two-hundred-year-old family tradition.

In all likelihood, the Mount Vernon Ladies' Association argues, West Ford was indeed the son of a Washington, but not of George Washington. "There is some pretty strong evidence suggesting that West Ford may have been the son of another member of the Washington family." To do a DNA test such as that done in the case of Jefferson-Hemmings, one would need to have DNA from at least one living male-line descendant of West Ford and one living male-line descendant of one of George Washington's brothers or other paternal relatives. If the Y-chromosomal DNA from these two individuals matched exactly or almost exactly, that would be strong evidence that a Washington—not necessarily George—was West Ford's father. In short, at the present development stage of DNA science, no direct link to George Washington can be established. The Mount Vernon Ladies' Association has pledged its cooperation with testing as DNA science progresses.

Another candidate son is one Thomas Posey. According to family lore, Thomas Posey was the illegitimate child of George Washington. Friends of the family who knew Posey claimed the physical similarities between the two were striking. For almost two generations, historians have argued the connection between Posey and Washington. The case appears flimsy. The Posey family were neighbors of Washington, living six miles away from Mount Vernon, but the two families were engaged more in business than social endeavors.

Thomas Posey was born on July 9, 1750. Posey described his parentage as being "respectable." He acknowledged his financial status as being "without fortune, but of tolerable English education." He set forth to find fame and fortune, which he did. Posey rose through the ranks of the military during the Revolution. After the Revolution, he rose to the rank of brigadier general and participated in Indian fighting in the Northwest. Posey served as a territorial governor for Indiana and then as an agent for Indian Affairs until his death in 1818.

So why is it that some people believe that Thomas Posey could have been an illegitimate child of George Washington? In 1871, the first published story of a possible direct heir to George Washington was printed in Indiana. The article detailed the family's oral tradition. The article indicated Posey's mother was a widow and had an illicit affair with Washington in 1754. Subsequent publications continued to use the same date as the first article, neglecting to cite the fact that Thomas Posey was actually born in 1750, four years before the alleged affair.

THE STRANGE CASE
OF HENRY WASHINGTON

Born on the Gambia River around 1740, Henry Washington (real name unknown) was captured and sold into slavery sometime before 1763. He subsequently became the property of George Washington and was a groom in the stables at Mount Vernon. In November 1775, the royal governor of Virginia, Lord Dunmore, issued a proclamation offering freedom to any slave who would help put down the American rebels. That December, George Washington, commanding the Continental army in Massachusetts, received a report from his cousin Lund that Lord Dunmore's proclamation had stirred the passions of Washington's own slaves. "There is not a man of them but would leave us if they believed they could make their escape. Liberty is sweet." In August 1776, a month after the signing of the Declaration of Independence, Henry Washington made his escape from Mount Vernon, making his way to the British lines and joining Lord Dunmore's all-Black "Ethiopian Regiment." With several hundred men under arms, the Ethiopian Regiment fought for the Crown and the freedom of all Blacks in slavery under the regimental motto "Liberty to Slaves." Lord Dunmore's forces were overwhelmed in Virginia, and the Ethiopian Regiment disbanded. Henry Washington went on to serve in another Loyalist regiment, the Black Pioneers, under the command of Sir Henry Clinton as they moved from New York to Philadelphia to Charleston and, after the fall of Charleston, back to New York.

Henry Washington was not alone in joining the British. The so-called Black Loyalists in the Revolutionary War are estimated to have numbered

Henry Washington escaped from Mount Vernon and fought for the British.

between 80,000 and 100,000 runaways who sought freedom within the lines of the British army. By freeing the slaves, the British forced slave masters to guard slaves, one of their chief economic assets, instead of fighting British troops. The British were willing to emancipate slaves if by so doing they could first cripple and then crush the rebellion. The use of slaves by the British for military purposes soon prompted the American rebels to begin recruiting Blacks. George Washington gave his approval to Rhode Island's plan to raise an entire regiment of Black slaves (the state bought and emancipated slaves willing to become soldiers). Similarly, Massachusetts raised an all-Black unit, the Bucks of America, under Samuel Middleton, the only Black commissioned officer in the Continental army. In October 1780, even Maryland accepted "any able-bodied slave between 16 and 40 years of age, who voluntarily enters into service…with the consent and agreement of his master." New York began recruiting slaves in March 1781. By June 1781 some 1,500 of the 6,000 troops under George Washington's direct command were Black.

In 1782, a provisional treaty granting the American colonies their independence was signed by Great Britain. As the British prepared for their final evacuation, the Americans demanded the return of runaway slaves under the terms of the peace treaty. The British refused to abandon Black Loyalists who had fought for the Crown to their fate. Some four thousand Blacks who had served the Crown during the war, together with their families, were listed in "The Book of Negroes." Those lucky enough to make the list sailed to freedom in Canada and England. Among them was Henry Washington.

Henry Washington embarked on the ship *L'Abondance* in July 1783 with 405 other Black Loyalists, including women and children, bound for Nova Scotia. He was forty-three years old. His wife, Jenny, was twenty-four. Most of the Black Loyalists on board *L'Abondance* were followers of a blind preacher called "Daddy Moses" who settled, as a community, in a place they named Birchtown.

Life in Nova Scotia was hard. The Crown was slow in allocating land, the weather was harsh and the soil was rocky and poor. After several unhappy years in Nova Scotia, Henry Washington, together with his wife and 3 children and 1,192 other Black colonists, joined an enterprise sponsored by the Sierra Leone Company (and financed by the British government) that allowed Black Loyalist refugees to join the free Black community established in Sierra Leone in West Africa. In 1791, Henry Washington and his family settled in Sierra Leone. New settlers were promised twenty acres for every man, ten for every woman and five for every child. They were also given assurances that in Sierra Leone there would be no discrimination between white and Black settlers.

The company was long on promises and short on delivery. Relations between the company and the colonists deteriorated to the point that the company sought a royal charter from the British parliament that would give the company formal jurisdiction over Sierra Leone. The company wanted full judicial authority to suppress dissent. The company explained, "The unwarranted pretensions of the disaffected settlers; their narrow misguided views; their excessive jealousy of Europeans; the crude notions they had formed of their own rights; and the impetuosity of their tempers" would soon produce a "ruinous effect."

The settlers, who regarded themselves as loyal British subjects, petitioned the king, explaining how the Black settlers had been given land by the British government as a consequence of "our good behavior in the last war." The king, hearing of their unhappiness about living in a cold country, offered to "remove us to Sierra Leone where we may be comfortable." Things had not turned out in accordance with the terms of

His Majesty's offer, and the settlers sought redress. The company ensured that the settlers' petition never reached the king.

By 1799, Sierra Leone's settlers had grown so discontented, so revolutionary in their rejection of the company's rule over the colony that some in London likened them to the revolutionaries in France. The company noted with alarm "meetings of a most seditious and dangerous nature." The governor sent armed marshals to arrest several men on charges of treason. Within a week, thirty-one men were in custody. A military tribunal was set up to try the prisoners for "open and unprovoked rebellion." Henry Washington and twenty-three others were banished to the colony's desolate northern shore.

The exiles elected Henry Washington their leader in 1800, only months after George Washington's death at Mount Vernon. In the love of liberty, Henry Washington was not excelled by the better-known George Washington.

LORD FAIRFAX AND
THE LOST AMERICAN PEERS

homas Fairfax was created Lord Fairfax of Cameron in the Peerage of Scotland on May 4, 1627. Another Thomas, the Sixth Lord Fairfax, succeeded to the title in 1709, at which time he came into the family estates in Virginia, some five million acres. The Sixth Lord Fairfax moved to Virginia to oversee the source of his wealth. Lord Fairfax was the only British peer to take up permanent residence in North America.

In 1748, Lord Fairfax employed the sixteen-year-old George Washington, a distant relative, to survey his lands in western Virginia. During the American Revolution, Lord Fairfax remained loyal to the Crown but did not leave America. His lands were confiscated, and the eighty-eight-year-old peer died less than two months after Washington's victory at Yorktown in 1781.

Lord Fairfax's title descended to his only surviving brother, Robert, who received cash compensation from the British Parliament for the loss of property during the Revolution. The settlement was a small fraction of the value of the confiscated land.

Robert died in 1793. An American cousin, Bryan Fairfax, claimed and was granted the title. Bryan Fairfax became the first American-born holder of a British peerage, although he did not actually use the title, choosing to become an Episcopal priest.

In 1802, Thomas Fairfax inherited the title Ninth Lord Fairfax of Cameron after his father's death. He lived the life of a country squire, overseeing his forty thousand acres. His grandson Charles succeeded to the title. Charles's brother John succeeded his childless brother, becoming the Eleventh Lord Fairfax of Cameron.

By the late nineteenth century, the family had largely forgotten about the title. This all soon changed. In 1900, Albert Kirby Fairfax succeeded his father. In 1901, he was summoned to attend the funeral of Victoria, the queen empress of the British Empire, ruler of one-quarter of the earth's territory and people. The Committee of Privileges of the House of Lords confirmed Albert Fairfax as the rightful Twelfth Lord Fairfax of Cameron. The newly recognized Lord Fairfax became a naturalized British subject on November 17, 1908. The family resettled in Britain after an interlude of some 150 years.

Nicholas John Albert Fairfax is now the Fourteenth Lord Fairfax of Cameron.

THE PAUL REVERE OF VIRGINIA

Virginia experienced a spate of military activity early in the Revolutionary War. Lord Dunmore, the royal governor, fought to keep the colony loyal to the Crown. Overconfident after an easy victory at Kemp's Landing, Lord Dunmore ordered an attack on Patriot forces near Norfolk. Only after a fierce battle ending in the destruction of Norfolk was Dunmore expelled. Lord Dunmore's army evacuated Norfolk, embarking on British ships. Smallpox broke out on the crowded ships even as the fleet left Virginia waters bound for New York.

Three years of relative peace followed. Virginia's false sense of security was rudely shattered in 1779 by a British expedition under Admiral Sir George Collier that raided and occupied the port cities of the Tidewater.

In 1781, the British stepped up operations in the southern theater of war. Benedict Arnold and a British fleet ravaged the Tidewater of Virginia, burning cities, seizing crops and destroying everything that they could find. In April, the British warship HMS *Savage* anchored off George Washington's plantation, Mount Vernon. The British raiders took seventeen of Washington's slaves. Lund Washington, a cousin who was watching over the plantation during the general's absence, went on board the *Savage*, took refreshments to the British officers and tried to negotiate the return of the slaves. He failed. A week later, the Marquis de Lafayette wrote to General Washington criticizing Lund's actions: "This being done by the gentleman who, in some measure, represents you at your house will certainly have a bad effect, and contrasts with spirited answers from some

Jack Jouett made a daring ride to Monticello and Charlottesville that saved Thomas Jefferson and the Virginia Assembly.

neighbors, that had their houses burnt accordingly." The general sent the unfortunate Lund a stinging letter rebuking him for "communing with a parcel of plundering Scoundrels."

Later in the year, Lord Cornwallis swept northward into Virginia and began to lay the country to waste. His only opposition was a small American force under the Frenchman Lafayette. The Virginia General Assembly abandoned Williamsburg, Richmond and Petersburg, fleeing to Charlottesville. The Virginia delegates decided to assemble in mid-June. The British hatched a plan to capture or kill the entire Virginia Assembly and Governor Thomas Jefferson in one lightning raid that would crush all opposition. Lord Cornwallis chose the savage Banastre Tarleton and his battle-hardened cavalry to do the job.

On the night of June 3, 1781, twenty-seven-year-old John "Jack" Jouett spotted Tarleton's cavalry near Cuckoo Tavern in Louisa County. Suspecting that the British were marching on Charlottesville, Jouett mounted his horse at 10:00 p.m. and began the forty-mile ride to Charlottesville. Traveling only with the light of the moon, Jouett took rough backwoods trails, riding hard to outdistance the British.

At 11:30 p.m., Tarleton paused for a three-hour rest at Louisa Courthouse. The British resumed their march at about 2:00 a.m. and soon encountered a train of thirteen Patriot supply wagons at Boswell's Tavern bound for South Carolina. Tarleton burned the wagons and continued toward Charlottesville.

At 4:30 a.m., Jack Jouett ascended the mountain on which Jefferson's home Monticello sits. An early riser, Thomas Jefferson was in the gardens at Monticello when Jouett arrived. Jefferson fortified Jouett with a glass of Madeira wine and sent him on the two additional miles to warn the town of Charlottesville.

Jefferson did not rush to make an escape. He had breakfast and spent two hours gathering up important papers, all the while checking the path up the mountain with his telescope for signs of the British. When Jefferson finally spotted the British, he mounted a horse and headed into the woods, successfully eluding capture.

Thanks to Jouett's timely warning, most of the Virginia legislators in Charlottesville also escaped capture. Tarleton only managed to capture seven assemblymen, whom he later released as being of no importance. One of these Virginia representatives was Daniel Boone.

1800 TO 1900

HENRY "BOX" BROWN

One of the most spectacular escapes from slavery made before the American Civil War was that of Henry Brown. Henry Brown was born into slavery in Louisa County in 1815. A clever lad, Henry was leased out to a tobacco factory in Richmond at the age of fifteen. The life of an urban slave was very different than that of a country slave. With the expansion of the industrial sector in Richmond, changes in slave living conditions occurred. Separate slave housing was common by the 1840s. Monitoring slave activities would have required constant supervision and thus was not done. Urban slave workers took to "losing time" when no one was watching. This practice was akin to rural "running away" and was a similar form of resistance. Many owners offered rewards as incentives not to "lose time" and even gave slaves an opportunity to pursue their own entrepreneurial ventures. Thus, Henry Brown was able to accumulate some money of his own.

Unfortunately, human greed continued to plague Henry Brown's existence. Henry had fallen in love and married a woman named Nancy, who lived on a country plantation near the one on which he was born. The couple had three children. Nancy's owner, aware that Henry was making money in Richmond, began to extort money from him in order to guarantee the "well-being" of Nancy and the children on his plantation. In 1848, when Nancy was pregnant with the couple's fourth child, Henry got the bad news: Nancy and the children were to be sold to a plantation in North Carolina. He would never see them again. With tears in his eyes, Henry watched as

Henry "Box" Brown made one of the cleverest and most spectacular escapes from slavery ever made.

350 chained slaves, including his wife and children, walked by him. "My agony was now complete, she with whom I had traveled the journey of life in chains…and the dear little pledges God had given us I could see plainly must now be separated from me forever, and I must continue, desolate and alone, to drag my chains through the world," Henry Brown later wrote.

After months of despair and desolation, Henry Brown hit on a desperate scheme to win his freedom. Through his faith in God, Brown later said, he was given the inspiration and courage to put together a creative plan of escape. "I conceived of a plan of shutting myself up in a box and getting myself conveyed as dry goods to a free state." Enlisting the help of a free Black friend and a white sympathizer, Samuel Smith, Henry Brown set about executing his plan.

Smith contacted James McKim, a white abolitionist and member of the Philadelphia Anti-Slavery Society. The abolitionists assured Smith that they were ready to receive Henry Brown in Philadelphia. Smith then procured a box three feet long by two feet eight inches deep by two feet wide and marked the box as "dry goods." The box had only three small air holes.

On the morning of March 29, 1849, Henry Brown crammed himself into the box carrying only an awl, in case he needed to drill more air holes, and a small flask of water. Brown's co-conspirators nailed the box shut, marked "This Side Up with Care" and carried the box to the Adams Express Company. Henry Brown's journey got off on its rocky way. Brown traveled by a variety of wagons, railroads, steamboats and ferries on the way to Philadelphia. The box was often roughly handled, and at one point, it was turned upside down. Brown wrote that he "was resolved to conquer or die, I felt my eyes swelling as if they would burst from their sockets; and the veins on my temples were dreadfully distended with pressure of blood upon my head." At one point, Brown relates, "I felt a cold sweat coming over me that seemed to be warning that death was about to terminate my earthly miseries." Fortunately, two men needed a place to sit down and, "so perceiving my box, standing on end, one of the men threw it down and the two sat upon it. I was thus relieved from a state of agony which may be more imagined than described."

After twenty-seven hours, the box arrived at its destination in Philadelphia. When the box was opened, a very much alive Henry Brown popped out and said to four astonished abolitionists, "How do you do, gentlemen?" He then recited a psalm: "I waited patiently on the Lord and He heard my prayer." Unable to contain his euphoria, Brown began to sing the psalm, to the delight of the abolitionists, who dubbed him Henry "Box" Brown.

Henry "Box" Brown became a sensation. He went on tour and thrilled audiences with the story of his daring escape. In May 1849, he appeared before the New England Anti-Slavery Society Convention in Boston, where he passionately made the case that the enslaved wanted freedom. He often recited the psalm he uttered when he emerged from his famous box when addressing audiences. In September 1849, the story of Henry "Box" Brown was published in Boston. Late in 1849, Brown had a moving panorama about slavery made. The panorama consisted of large vertical spools painted with scenes of enslavement and freedom and was called *Henry Box Brown's Mirror of Slavery*.

Henry Brown sailed to England in October 1850. His panorama was exhibited all over England. At this point, Brown, a natural performer, left the abolitionist circuit and totally embraced show business for the next forty years, performing as an actor, singer and magician in England, the United States and Canada. Brown's last performance took place in Brantford, Ontario, Canada, on February 26, 1889. Henry "Box" Brown died in Toronto on June 15, 1897.

THE STRANGE FATE
OF WILMER McLEAN

Wilmer McLean was born in 1814, was orphaned before he was nine, was raised by relatives in Alexandria and became a prosperous food merchant in Alexandria. In 1853, he married Virginia Hooe Mason, a wealthy widow with extensive real estate holdings and other property. She owned Yorkshire plantation in Prince William County, estimated to have some 1,200 acres; a tract of 330 acres in Fairfax County; and two other tracts containing 500 acres in Prince William County. She also owned fourteen slaves. There were two daughters by her first marriage, Maria (born 1844) and Osceola (born 1845). Both girls lived with the Wilmer McLeans at Manassas and were described as McLean's "two pretty daughters." Two other children were born of the McLean marriage, Wilmer McLean Jr. (born 1854) and Lucretia Virginia (born 1857).

Following the First Battle of Manassas, Mrs. McLean and the children left the area. Wilmer McLean, however, worked diligently as a civilian with the Confederate Quartermaster Department. He worked to expedite the flow of food supplies to the troops in camp near Manassas. There was a time when the troops were down to one day's rations. McLean's experience as a wholesale merchant was invaluable in solving the problem of purchasing supplies in the fertile country around Manassas.

McLean's most valuable contribution to the Confederacy was agreeing to let the army take over the buildings of Yorkshire plantation for use as a military hospital. The barn was used as a hospital, and the main house and outbuildings were used as living quarters for the surgeons and hospital attendants from July 17, 1861, until February 28, 1862. By 1862, however, McLean was completely disenchanted by the misconduct of soldiers and hospital personnel at Yorkshire. Large quantities of wine and whiskey were consumed by the hospital attendants. Sanitation was woefully lacking; flies covered the faces of patients. The house and outbuildings were grossly mistreated while occupied by surgeons and attendants.

Further evidence of his disillusionment was his growing price demands on the quartermaster. McLean apparently purchased candles and other scarce items in Richmond, had them shipped to Manassas and then sold them to the Confederate quartermaster for the highest price he could get.

When the Confederate army marched out of Northern Virginia in March 1862, Mclean left the area permanently, moving his family and household goods to central Virginia, far from the sound of battle. From his experience as a merchant, McLean knew that a long war would cause the price of commodities to rise higher and higher. He began speculating in sugar and made a tidy income during the war. By the end of the war, however, McLean, like most Virginians, was virtually penniless. The McLeans still owned hundreds of acres of land in Northern Virginia, but the land was virtually worthless for resale, and McLean was heavily in debt.

Eventually, the ever-practical McLean turned his attention to politics. He joined the Yankee Republican Party, supported Grant in the election of 1872 and was rewarded by an appointment to a U.S. Treasury job.

These are the bare facts of Wilmer McLean's life; he was a family man, a shrewd merchant and a resourceful survivor. But fate was to take a hand in Wilmer McLean's life, making him one of the most unusual characters in American history, for the Civil War virtually began in his kitchen in Manassas and ended in his front parlor at Appomattox Court House. On July 18, 1861, the advancing Union army began probing Confederate defenses along Bull Run Creek at a place called Blackburn's Ford. General Beauregard, the Confederate commander, set up headquarters at Yorkshire, the Mcleans' home, to keep a closer eye on the Union army. About noon, an artillery duel started. One of the Union shells smashed into the chimney of the McLean house. Dropping down the chimney, the shell exploded in a big iron kettle simmering on the fire, plastering the kitchen with stew meant for dinner. Miraculously, no one was injured. As earlier noted, McLean and his family moved in March 1862 to central Virginia, where they were immune to the sights and sounds of war for three years. On the morning of April 9, 1865, however, two horsemen—one Federal and one Confederate— ordered McLean to conduct them to some house with a large room where

The Civil War began in McLean's kitchen in Manassas and ended in his front parlor at Appomattox (seen here).

a conference could be held. After taking them to several houses, McLean finally took them to his own house. The two officers chose McLean's house for the historic meeting between Generals Lee and Grant where General Lee surrendered the Army of Northern Virginia. Over the next few days, souvenir hunters from the Union army virtually gutted the parlor in the rush for mementos of the historic occasion.

THE LEGEND OF MOSBY'S LOST LOOT

N orth central Virginia became the preserve of one of the most dashing figures of the Civil War, John Singleton Mosby. Mosby grew up in the shadow of the central Blue Ridge, attended the University of Virginia and practiced law in southwest Virginia. He signed up for the Confederate service shortly after the firing at Fort Sumter. By the summer of 1861, he was part of "Jeb" Stuart's cavalry. He served as Stuart's scout throughout much of 1862 and accompanied him on his Fairfax raid in December of that year. When Stuart rode out of Fairfax County, Mosby, with nine men, had permission to remain behind.

Northern Virginia was a region of small and scattered communities set amid gently rolling hills. It was an ideal area for cavalry operations, and in the last three years of the war, Mosby's horsemen so dominated activities in the area that it was often called "Mosby's Confederacy." Mosby was everywhere. He destroyed railway tracks. He robbed sutlers and Union paymasters. He captured pickets and shot down stragglers. Mosby, with a price on his head, crossed Long Bridge into Washington City in the full light of day. In Washington, he hobnobbed with Union officers at the bar of a crowded hotel, slept in a bed next to one of them and returned unharmed to Virginia. Mosby stopped ladies on their way to Washington and sent a lock of his hair to President Lincoln.

With less than 250 men, Mosby immobilized 30,000 Union troops and kept them from front-line duty. His command, often consisting of fewer than 50 men, captured thousands of Union troops, horses and mules.

John Singleton Mosby was one of the most dashing figures of the Civil War.

The Union army camped around Washington in a gigantic protective circle. Well beyond the main army camps, a great ring of picket posts was established. Mosby began eliminating these first. On dark nights, his men would slip into and around these isolated posts, where, if seen, they were taken for Union troops. Then, on a given signal, the Confederates would suddenly rush in with their revolvers, cover the small Union garrison and, most often without firing a shot, take them prisoner and confiscate their arms and horses. Mosby's little command began an almost daily series of small raids.

Soon civilians in the area became conscious of the Mosby magic, and many offered to enlist under the Virginia law that authorized the creation of guerrilla bands. While the Confederacy regarded Mosby and his irregulars as patriots, from the viewpoint of Washington and the Federal troops, the guerrillas were no better than highway robbers—a character that was substantiated by the fact that under Virginia law, Mosby's guerrillas were permitted to keep the spoils they seized from the Union.

Mosby's most daring exploit was the capture of General Edwin H. Stoughton in Fairfax Court House. Stoughton, the son of a prominent Vermont politician, had been made a brigadier general before his twenty-fifth birthday. The general loved rich living and beautiful women and surrounded himself with both in the comfortable two-story brick residence that he set up as his headquarters. Around him, quartered in other homes of the community, were his aides, couriers and a guard of two hundred men. All the conveniences allowed an outpost officer were his. There were fine horses, carriages, silver, servants and the finest food and wine.

One chilly March night, as heavy rains pelted the pickets who had been purposefully stationed far from the general headquarters, Stoughton entertained a glittering assembly of beautiful women, brother officers and foreign visitors. Dancing and gaiety abounded, and the champagne flowed freely. Soon, the rolling hills around Fairfax Court House echoed with the sounds of merriment.

Midnight approached. The gaiety grew louder and the guests more oblivious to the war and weather conditions outside. After all, the nearest Rebel forces were twenty-five miles away, there was the line of pickets to prevent a sudden dash on headquarters and the Virginia mud was so thick that it made an attack out of the question.

At 2:00 a.m., the last reveler fell into bed. Then came the noises of cavalry splashing in on the soupy road. The picket in the center of the village heard the horses but continued to walk his beat. That would be Yankee horsemen; no Rebel troops could be within miles.

The horsemen, thirty in all, rode into town and divided into three groups. The picket continued his tiresome tread. He was concerned but not alarmed. And then, in the drizzling faintness of the lamp, he found himself staring at the barrel of a big Colt six-shooter.

Lieutenant Prentiss, Stoughton's aide, was awakened by shouts that there were dispatches outside for the general. When the aide opened the door, six men walked in, and a small, wiry man with a plume in his hat stuck a gun in the aide's ribs while the aide stood in the hallway in shirt drawers holding high a smoking oil lamp.

Upstairs, the be-plumed Mosby walked into the bedroom of the half-drunk General Stoughton and pulled down the blankets. The brigadier was lying on his side, snoring, but he roused up stupidly when Mosby lifted his nightshirt and slapped him on the behind.

"Get up, General, and come with me."

The sound of a voice brought Stoughton more fully awake. When he realized the man bending over him was a stranger, he roared: "What is this? Do you know who I am, sir?"

"I reckon I do, General. Did you ever hear of Mosby?"

"Yes, have you caught him?"

"No, but he has caught you."

As Mosby's raiders rode out of Fairfax Court House, they took with them, besides General Stoughton, two captains, thirty privates, fifty-eight horses and $350,000 (now valued at several million) worth of gold plate, jewelry, silver tableware and gold coins that Stoughton had looted from neighboring Southern homes. Mosby marched his prisoners to Culpepper, where they were turned over to General J.E.B. Stuart.

About midway between Haymarket and New Baltimore, Mosby, accompanied by only one sergeant, James F. Ames (who was captured and hanged by Union general George Custer a short time later), is said to have buried the loot between two pine trees, marking the trees with knives.

Mosby continued his activities unabated right to the end of the war, when he gathered his men one last time and disbanded, never officially surrendering to Federal forces.

Mosby went on to become a distinguished railway lawyer (and attorney to the father of George S. Patton). Shortly before his death in 1916, at the age of eighty-three, he told some of his close friends, "I've always meant to look for that cache we buried after capturing Stoughton. Some of the most precious heirlooms of old Virginia are in that sack. I guess that one of these days someone will find it."

THE LOST CONFEDERATE TREASURY

April 2, 1865, was a Sunday, and in Richmond, Jefferson Davis was at church. In the midst of the services, a courier arrived with a message from the War Department: "General Lee telegraphs he can hold his position no longer." Davis quietly left the church and set about removing his government from Richmond.

One of the principal concerns of the fleeing Confederate government was the evacuation of the treasury. Despite months of siege, very little preparation had been made for an orderly evacuation of Richmond. Mann Quarles, the youngest teller in the Confederate Treasury, relates:

> We were instructed to pack and be in readiness to take an R&D train on quick notice. This we commenced to do. A large part of the force went to their respective homes in the city to individually prepare to leave, leaving the brunt of the packing of the coin and really valuable things with but a few of us....Observing that no account was being kept of the contents of the respective boxes, I took several large sheets of brown paper....On each page of this...I wrote a description of the marks on each box and stated the content of the same on such page.

Before the last official left the treasury, they kept the furnace in the basement of the building red-hot with burning Confederate notes, bonds and papers.

It is interesting to note that no proper accounting was made of the Confederate Treasury. This no doubt accounts for the widely varying accounts of its size, which run from $500,000 in gold and silver to well over $20,000,000. Rumors persist that not all of the treasury made it out on the great treasure train. Local legends assert that $10 million in gold coins and bullion lent to the Confederacy by Great Britain was buried along the banks of the James River near Berkeley Plantation, just east of Hopewell. Another legend tells of $3 million in gold bullion buried along the banks of the James River about two miles south of the city.

Whatever the truth of these legends, it is certain that as news of Lee's imminent retreat spread, panic gripped the city. All over the city it was the same: wagons, trunks, bandboxes and their owners—a mass of hurrying fugitives filling the streets. The banks were all open, and depositors stampeded to remove their specie deposits. The bank directors were equally active in getting their bullion off. Much of the gold taken from the banks was buried or sent elsewhere for safekeeping. Emmie Crump, an eyewitness to the fall of Richmond, recounts:

> *We sent for him* [a freed slave] *and gave him many valuables to care for at his house; my sister, two little brothers and myself carried what we could of silver to our Aunt's house as we were advised to do. My mother made some strong belts and put into them as much gold coin as we could conveniently carry and wore them under our clothing.*

By late afternoon, it seemed that all who could leave the city were stampeding. Commissary stores were thrown open and their hoarded contents distributed to eager crowds. And strange crowds they were. Fragile, delicate women staggered under heavy loads they bore to suffering children at home; children cried for what they could carry; and white-haired old men tugged wearily at barrels of pork, flour and sugar.

As the day wore on, the scenes at the various government stores changed from the fairly orderly distribution of supplies to rank plundering. Whiskey stocks were broken into, and the streets ran with liquor.

Factories, arsenals and mills were ordered destroyed. Some were blown up, while others were burned, and the fires were soon out of control. The panic was extreme. Men, women and children hurried to and fro. Commissary stores were destroyed. The streets were blocked with men and beasts. Fierce crowds of skulking men and coarse, half-drunken women gathered, breaking into shops and fighting among themselves over the spoils they

Large sections of Richmond were destroyed in 1865 as fire ravaged the city.

seized. Through the night, drunken mobs of civilians and army deserters roamed the city, looting and burning.

Captain Parker, of the Confederate navy, made his way through the crowds escorting the Confederate Treasury. The gold coins and other valuables of the treasury were brought to the train depot in kegs and boxes. Gold double eagles, gold ingots, Mexican silver dollars and silver bricks were packed into railway cars.

The great Confederate treasure train was scheduled as "the last out of the city." The train first went to Danville and then to Greensboro, North Carolina. The treasure next moved farther south by wagon train. Finally, the treasure, transported in small iron chests, money belts, shot bags and boxes, caught up with the fleeing Jefferson Davis in Washington, Georgia.

At this point, the treasure was apportioned. The monies belonging to the Richmond banks were given to the proper agents. Some money was split among Confederate troops as compensation for back pay that they had never received. Some of the gold was concealed in the false bottom of a carriage to be smuggled to a ship, where it would be shipped to a Confederate agent in Nassau for the Confederate government's account. The remaining treasure was repacked aboard two wagons along with Davis's personal baggage consisting of a trunk and two chests. Captain M.C. Clark was placed in command of the wagons. In Clark's guard of eight was one Tench F. Tilghman.

At Sandersville, Georgia, the party split once again. Clark led the treasure wagons toward Madison, Florida, while Davis turned southwest. On the morning of May 10, a marauding Union cavalry party captured Jefferson Davis near Irwinville, Georgia.

The news of President Davis's capture did not reach the treasure train immediately. The caravan continued on for another week, crossing the Witlacoochee River into Florida on May 15.

On May 22, 1865, news of the president's capture reached the tiny command encamped northwest of Gainesville, near a large plantation. Final defeat was now at hand. Captain Clark divided the money in the wagon among his men and then dispersed the troops. Before Tilghman left Gainesville, however, he buried his portion of the money plus the government archives and Jefferson Davis's personal papers. Other men also buried their shares.

Two years later, Tench Tilghman was at the Astor House in New York City attending a convention. He met William L. Stone, an old friend, and told him that he alone buried the treasure and the archives that had been entrusted to his care. Tilghman claimed that everything was still where he had buried it. Four days later, Tilghman suffered a violent hemorrhage and died without revealing the site of the treasure or, what is today probably more valuable, the cache of Davis's personal papers.

VIRGINIA RAILROAD LORE

The first American steam locomotive was built in 1825. Two years later, the Baltimore and Ohio Railroad became the first railway in the United States chartered for commercial passenger use. In 1836, the Louisa Railroad was chartered in Virginia, and on December 20, 1837, the first forty-seven-mile line was completed between Richmond and Fredericks Hall in Louisa County. The crowd on opening day gasped, "Who could have expected to see this?"

Virginia's early railroads were not designed to be a transportation network. The railroads were locally owned and designed to transport inland farm products, timber and iron to specific ports. In 1859, the city of Alexandria, for example, received ninety-one thousand bushels of wheat from rural Virginia destined for shipment to other ports, making it the second-largest wheat exporting center in Virginia. At the same time freight cars were bringing agricultural products into Alexandria for shipment, freight trains laden with guano fertilizer from South America moved inland from the city. This imported fertilizer was the key to a resurgence of agricultural exports in Virginia.

During the Civil War, the Confederacy was quick to utilize railroads, bringing troops from the Shenandoah Valley to Manassas in July 1861. At the most critical phase of the First Battle of Manassas, the Thirty-Third Virginia Infantry Regiment detrained at Manassas Junction and marched to the sound of the guns. At this point in the war, both armies were clothed and equipped in an irregular and eccentric manner. The Thirty-Third Virginia was dressed not in gray but in blue. The Federals were fooled and did not realize their mistake until the Virginians crashed into their flank, winning the battle for the Confederacy. Two cities in Virginia exist solely because of railroad junctions. Manassas and Roanoke grew from the start as towns where two railroads connected.

At the time of the Civil War, railroads were still a novelty. In August 1862, boxcars packed with military supplies were sitting in Washington. The supplies could not be moved across the Potomac River into Virginia because authorities were afraid that available locomotives were too heavy for the rickety railroad bridge across the Potomac. The Union army's Brigadier General Herman Haupt, a railroad construction engineer, revolutionized military transportation and was one of the unsung heroes of the Civil War. Trains traveled five times faster than mule-drawn wagons, which reduced the number of supply vehicles required. Faster travel meant cargoes arrived at the front in better condition. Troops traveling by train experienced less fatigue. Because of Haupt's innovations, Union railroads boosted logistical output by at least a factor of ten, having a profound impact on the outcome of the Civil War.

Haupt's nemesis was the Confederate raider John S. Mosby, who delighted in attacking the railroads. A single stretch of track of the Orange and Alexandria Railroad connected the Union army, moving on Richmond, to the vast supply depots of Alexandria and Washington. At various times, Mosby's raiders cut telegraph lines, tore up rails and destroyed railway bridges along this critical stretch of track. Explosive devices planted in the roadbed posed serious threats to trains. Mines were often artillery shells with percussion fuses. Buried in the roadbed, mines would be detonated by a passing train. Mines, especially those using artillery shells, could lift locomotives off the tracks.

Keeping the trains running was an enormous task and essential for victory. General Haupt sent out crews and a construction train to repair damaged tracks and bridges. The Construction Corps was responsible for making rail lines fit for military use. It consisted of professional civil engineers, skilled workmen and manual laborers who were provided with materials, tools and their own transport. Among their materials were prefabricated tracks and bridges needed to quickly replace tracks and bridges destroyed by raiders.

When the trains were running, they carried supplies and rations for the army and were heavily guarded by riflemen sitting on top of the railroad cars. Union officers armored some engines against snipers. Unfortunately, train crews found that armor limited their ability to escape from the engine

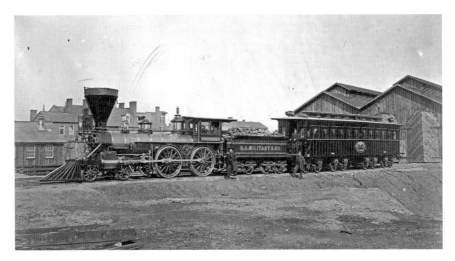

President Lincoln's private rail car, the Air Force One of its day, was built in Virginia.

in case of emergencies, an important consideration, since a ruptured boiler could fatally scald a crew. In October 1864, a number of prominent citizens known to be Confederate sympathizers were forced to ride military trains as human shields.

Although the size and tempo of railroad operations greatly increased during the war years, even before the war Alexandria was home to the Smith and Perkins Locomotive Works. In the spring of 1865, a private railroad car was built for President Lincoln's personal use. This was the Air Force One of its day. Ironically, this special presidential car was used for the first time as a funeral car to take the slain President Lincoln back to his home in Springfield, Illinois. Lincoln's funeral train left Washington on April 21, 1865. It retraced much of the route Lincoln had traveled as president-elect in 1861. The nine-car Lincoln Special, whose engine had Lincoln's photograph over the cowcatcher, carried approximately three hundred mourners. Depending on conditions, the train usually traveled between five and twenty miles per hour.

After the Civil War, railroad ownership was consolidated, and people and freight began to move seamlessly throughout the state. The next seventy years marked the heyday of rail traffic in Virginia. Two spectacular train wrecks during this period contributed to Virginia's railroad lore.

Seventeen-year-old Myrtle Ruth Knox had recently joined a company of opera performers and was dreaming of a successful musical career. Her dreams were cut short on April 26, 1890, when her train crashed into the train depot in Staunton. The tracks west of Staunton drop eighty feet before reaching the train station. Two miles into the steep downgrade, the train's brakes were applied, but nothing happened. The train did not slow down; in fact, it went even faster. The cars shook violently until the train jumped the tracks and slammed into Staunton's train depot. The building collapsed and toppled over into the railway cars. Miraculously, there was only one fatality, young Myrtle Ruth Knox. A new station was built in 1902, only to be abandoned in 1960. The structure has since been the home of a number of restaurants. The ghost of Myrtle Ruth Knox is said to wander around the station's platform.

Virginia's most spectacular rail disaster inspired the famous railroad ballad "The Wreck of the Old 97." On September 27, 1903, the Southern Railway train number 97, the so-called Fast Mail, was running behind schedule. The Fast Mail had a reputation for never being late. Railroad company mangers instructed the train's engineer, Joseph A. Broady, to get that train back on schedule and make up the one hour he was running behind (the company had a contract with the government that included a financial penalty for every minute the train was late reaching its destination). Steep grades and tight curves made many places along the route potentially dangerous. Signs were posted along the way warning engineers to slow down. But Broady disregarded the signs and took one particularly steep grade at excessive speed. Because he was going too fast, Broady couldn't reduce his speed before reaching the curve leading into the Stillhouse Trestle near Danville. The 97, the Fast Mail, derailed and plunged into the ravine below. The train exploded in flames. Eleven people died, including Broady.

The disaster served as inspiration for songwriters and singers for generations, and "The Wreck of the Old 97" became one of the most popular railroading songs of all time. While railway company officials placed blame for the wreck on Broady, denying that he had been ordered to run at unsafe speeds, the ballad disagrees and begins, "Well, they handed him his orders in Monroe, Virginia, saying, 'Steve, you're way behind time; this is not 38 it is Old 97, you must put her into Spencer on time.'"

LEGENDARY WOMEN

POCAHONTAS AND CAPTAIN JOHN SMITH

Two of Virginia's most unusual and colorful characters were Captain John Smith and the Native American princess Pocahontas.

Captain John Smith was an English soldier of fortune who fought his way across Europe in wars being waged by the various rulers in Slovenia, Hungary and Transylvania, earning many awards for bravery. The prince of Transylvania awarded Smith a title and his own coat of arms, which displayed drawings of the heads of the three Turks killed and beheaded by Smith in individual combat. In 1602, Smith was wounded in battle and captured by the Turks. He was sold into slavery and marched six hundred miles to Constantinople. There, Smith was presented to his new master's fiancée as a gift. The woman promptly fell in love with Smith and tried to convert him to Islam. When this didn't work, she shipped him off to her brother in Rostov in what was then Turkish-occupied Russia.

The brother beat Smith frequently and put an iron collar around his neck. John Smith was a man who required a great deal of breaking, and his new master did not succeed. In fact, Smith killed him and escaped on his horse. With the help of local Christians, Smith traversed Russia and Ukraine, making his way to Germany, France and finally England. After traveling some eleven thousand miles between 1600 and 1604, you would think that Smith would be done with long journeys, but his longest journey was just about to begin.

In April 1606, the Virginia Company was granted a royal charter by King James I to establish a colony. In December, three ships carrying 104 settlers,

Ætatis suæ 21 Aº.1616.

Matoaks als Rebecka daughter to the mighty Prince Powhatan Emperour of Attanoughkomouck als Virginia converted and baptized in the Chriftian faith and Wife to the wor.ll Mr Tho: Rolff.

Pocahontas was hailed in both Virginia and England as a princess. She lived a remarkable life.

including Captain John Smith, set sail for Virginia. Impressed by Smith's military record, the Virginia Company invited Smith to join the enterprise as a member of the new colony's 7-man ruling council.

Jamestown, the first permanent English settlement in North America, named in honor of King James I, was founded on May 14, 1607. The early going was tough for the colonists. The colony suffered from food shortages, disease and unhealthy drinking water, all in addition to skirmishes with the local Powhatan tribe. In the autumn of 1607, Captain Smith conducted trips to Powhatan villages to secure much-needed food. During one of these forays, Smith was taken prisoner by a large Powhatan hunting party and ultimately brought before Wahunsenacawh, better known to history as Chief Powhatan.

According to Smith, his head was placed on two stones, and as he was held down, a warrior prepared to smash in his skull with a heavy club. Before the fatal blow fell, however, Chief Powhatan's daughter Pocahontas rushed to Smith's side and placed her head on his, preventing the attack. Thus was born the legend of the beautiful princess saving the life of the intrepid English adventurer.

It is easy to understand how Smith, unfamiliar with Powhatan customs, thought he was about to be murdered when, in fact, he was being inducted into the tribe. According to some anthropologists, Smith was undergoing a ritual adoption ceremony, and after the ceremony, he was treated well and ultimately returned to Jamestown. As for the Native American princess, her real name was Amonute (she also had the more private name Matoaka). Pocahontas was a nickname that meant "playful one." Did she really save John Smith? Smith only wrote of the incident years later when he was safely back in Europe and there was no one around to contradict his version. Some have suggested that he took the story of the hero being saved by the beautiful daughter of a powerful lord from an old Scottish ballad.

Whatever the truth of the rescue story, Pocahontas lived a remarkable life. While Smith was with the Powhatan tribe, he spent time with Pocahontas, and they taught each other rudimentary aspects of their different languages. Pocahontas became an important emissary to the Jamestown colony, negotiating the release of prisoners and occasionally bringing food to the hungry settlers. Notwithstanding her efforts, relations between the colonists and the Powhatan tribe remained strained. In 1609, the starving colonists threatened to burn Powhatan villages unless the tribe brought them food. Chief Powhatan offered to barter for food with Captain John Smith. Supposedly, the chief intended to ambush and kill Smith, but Pocahontas warned Smith of the plot and saved his life (again?). Smith returned to England after this incident.

Pocahontas avoided the English until 1613, when she was kidnapped. The English informed Chief Powhatan that Pocahontas would not be returned unless a food ransom was paid and certain stolen weapons returned. The ransom was slow in coming, and Pocahontas remained a prisoner in the settlement of Henricus, where she was under the care of a minister. Here she learned how to speak English and learned about both Christianity and European culture. Pocahontas converted to Christianity and took a new name, Rebecca.

After she had been a prisoner for a year, Sir Thomas Dale, with 150 armed men, marched Pocahontas to Chief Powhatan to demand the rest of the ransom. Along the way, a number of villages were burned and a skirmish occurred, but Pocahontas was able to secure peace when she announced to Chief Powhatan that she wished to marry one of the colonists, one John Rolfe, a tobacco planter. The chief agreed, and on April 5, 1614, the marriage took place, cementing the so-called Peace of Pocahontas.

In 1616, Sir Thomas Dale sailed for England to raise money and to demonstrate that the goal of converting Native Americans to Christianity was being met. John Rolfe, Pocahontas, their baby son Thomas (born in 1615) and twelve Powhatan tribe members made the trip. In London, Pocahontas was hailed as a princess and was presented to King James I. The Virginia Company commissioned a portrait of Pocahontas in European dress. The painting's identifying plaque reads, "Matoaka, alias Rebecca, daughter of the most powerful prince of the Powhatan Empire of Virginia."

In 1617, Pocahontas and her family set sail for Virginia but had hardly launched when she was overcome by a grave illness. The party disembarked at Gravesend, England, where she died. On her deathbed, she said, "All must die. But 'tis enough that my child liveth."

THE WITCH OF PUNGO

The most famous American witch trials occurred in Salem, Massachusetts, in 1692–93, but Virginia had its own witches and witch trials. All right-minded people in the American colonies took the existence of witches for granted. The devil was always a real and present danger. Despite being on constant alert and ever vigilant, Virginians did not experience the same degree of hysteria with regard to witches that gripped the Puritans of Massachusetts. For one thing, clerical influence was much less a factor in Virginia, where the clergy rarely participated in witchcraft trials. Unlike New England's witch trial courts, where the accused had to prove their innocence, in Virginia, the accuser had to demonstrate the accused was guilty. Nineteen witchcraft trials were held in Virginia during the seventeenth century. Most ended in the accused witch being acquitted. In a 1656 case, a man was convicted of witchcraft and sentenced to whipping and banishment. There was no death penalty for witchcraft in Virginia. The last witchcraft trial in Virginia took place in 1802.

Virginia's most famous witch, the so-called Witch of Pungo, was one Grace Sherwood, a forty-six-year-old married woman from Princess Anne County. Grace was married to James Sherwood, a planter. The couple had three sons: John, James and Richard. The family lived in Pungo (today part of Virginia Beach). Grace Sherwood was a strong woman, a healer and an herbalist and someone with an affinity for nature and animals. She did not suffer fools easily. This, at that time, was a sure formula for trouble with the neighbors. And trouble she got.

All right-minded people in the American colonies took the existence of witches for granted.

In early 1697, Richard Capps accused Grace of casting a spell that caused the death of his bull. The court found insufficient evidence of witchcraft, and the charge was dismissed. The Sherwoods sued Capps for slander. This case also went nowhere. The following year, John Gisburne accused Grace of casting a spell on his pigs and cotton crop. This resulted in another case of insufficient evidence and another failed defamation suit on the part of the Sherwoods. The year 1698 was a busy one for Grace Sherwood. Having beaten back the accusations of John Gisburne early in 1698, later in that year she was accused by Elizabeth Barnes of having assumed the shape of a black cat. As a demonic cat, Grace was accused of having entered the Barneses' home in the night, where she proceeded to jump over the bed and whip Elizabeth Barnes. The witch then left through the keyhole. Not surprisingly, this resulted in another case dismissed and another failed defamation suit on the part of the Sherwoods.

Things remained quiet for a number of years until, in 1705, Grace Sherwood was involved in a fight with her neighbor Elizabeth Hill. Sherwood sued Hill and her husband for assault and battery and was awarded monetary compensation in December 1705. This ruling by the court did nothing to calm tempers. On January 3, 1706, Elizabeth Hill accused Grace Sherwood of witchcraft, of having used her satanic powers to cause a miscarriage. In March 1706, the court ordered Sherwood's house to be searched for waxen or baked figures that might indicate she was a witch. No luck there; the search produced nothing. The court next authorized a jury of twelve women to look for marks of the devil on Grace Sherwood's body. The forewoman of this jury was the same Elizabeth Barnes who had previously accused Sherwood of witchcraft. Not surprisingly, this group discovered marks of the devil.

Despite this overwhelming evidence, authorities remained reluctant to declare Grace Sherwood a witch. Authorities in Williamsburg, the colonial capital, considered the charge against Sherwood too vague and ordered the local court to examine the case in greater depth.

By July, Grace Sherwood was worn out with traveling from her farm to court and thus consented when the court offered her a trial by ducking. The procedure here involved binding Grace and throwing her into the river; if she sank, she was innocent, but if she floated, she was clearly a witch.

Grace Sherwood's protestation that "I be not a witch, I be a healer," fell on deaf ears. People had come in from all over the colony to watch the spectacle. The crowd began to chant, "Duck the witch." A spot on the Lynnhaven River, now known as Witchduck Point, was chosen for the test. Grace Sherwood was securely bound, rowed out into the river and thrown from the boat. She rose to the surface—proof positive that she was a witch. The court, with an overabundance of judicial caution, decided to give Grace a second chance to demonstrate her innocence. The sheriff was ordered to tie a thirteen-pound Bible around her neck. Grace was rowed back to the middle of the river and thrown from the boat. Weighted down by the Bible, she sank but somehow managed to untie herself and return to the surface. She was definitely a witch, if there ever was one.

Grace Sherwood was convicted of witchcraft and sentenced to imprisonment. Freed from prison by 1714, Grace returned to her home and lived peacefully until her death in 1740. Some neighbors said the devil took her body. Others pointed to the increase in unnatural storms and loitering black cats after her death. Locals killed every cat they could find, which then led to an infestation of rats in 1743.

Grace Sherwood lies in an unmarked grave in a field near the intersection of Pungo Ferry Road and Princess Anne Road in Virginia Beach. To this day, local residents tell of a mysterious moving light that appears each July over the spot where Sherwood was thrown into the water. Is it possible that this is the restless spirit of Grace Sherwood? Perhaps, but not everyone is convinced that Grace Sherwood was a witch. The governor of Virginia granted her a pardon on July 10, 2006. Additionally, a statue of Grace Sherwood was erected on Independence Boulevard in Virginia Beach. Grace is shown alongside a raccoon, representing her love of animals, and carrying a basket containing garlic and rosemary, in recognition of her knowledge of herbal healing.

THE FEMALE STRANGER

Perhaps the most romantic tombstone in Virginia is that of Alexandria's "Female Stranger." In September 1816, a young couple arrived in Alexandria. The lady was very ill. She remained in her room at a local inn until her death. After her death, her husband erected a tomb, left the city and was never seen again. Her tombstone reads:

To the Memory of a
FEMALE STRANGER
whose mortal sufferings terminated
on the 14th day of October 1816
Aged 23 years and 8 months.
This stone is placed here by her disconsolate
Husband in whose arms she sighed out her
latest breath and who under God
did his utmost even to soothe the cold
dead ear of death.
How loved how valued once avails thee not
To whom related or by whom begot
A heap of dust alone remains of thee
'Tis all thou art and all the proud shall be.
To him gave all the Prophets witness that
through his name whosoever believeth in
him shall receive remission of sins.
Acts. 10th Chap. 43rd verse

Perhaps the most romantic tombstone in Virginia is that of Alexandria's "Female Stranger." *Author's collection.*

The identity of the Female Stranger remains a mystery. What secret did the young couple hide? Were they eloping? Was she an English aristocrat, royalty, the daughter of a prominent politician? The mystery lingers beyond the grave, but some have linked the Female Stranger to the disappearance of Theodosia Burr Alston.

The disappearance of Theodosia Burr Alston, the daughter of disgraced U.S. vice president Aaron Burr, is one of history's continuing mysteries. Theodosia was considered an intellectual prodigy in a time when women rarely received anything but a marginal education. At the age of eighteen, she married James Alston, who would become the forty-fourth governor of South Carolina. In 1807, her father, Aaron Burr, was tried for treason and, although found innocent, went into self-imposed exile. Theodosia acted as Burr's agent in America, raising money and raising support among the political elite for his return to America.

In December 1812, Theodosia boarded the schooner *Patriot* bound from South Carolina to New York. Neither Theodosia nor anyone onboard the *Patriot* was ever heard from again. Legend has surrounded her disappearance ever since, including tales that: (1) she was captured by pirates and became the mistress of a pirate captain; (2) she was made to "walk the plank" by the pirate Dominique Youx; (3) she was discovered by a Karankawa Indian chief on the Texas Gulf coast in the hulk of a wrecked ship but died before she could be returned to civilization; and (4) Theodosia Burr Alston may have been the mysterious Female Stranger who died in Alexandria, Virginia, at Gadsby's Tavern on October 14, 1816.

THE UNION SPY IN THE CONFEDERATE WHITE HOUSE

Elizabeth Van Lew of Richmond, although from an old Virginia family, was an ardent Unionist who refused to leave town even as the Confederate government took up residence. Her continued devotion to the Union cause was considered just another of the eccentricities of the woman her neighbors came to call "Crazy Bet." Van Lew began to accentuate her eccentricities. As she walked along the street, she mumbled and hummed to herself, head bent to one side, holding imaginary conversations. Her disguise served her well as she set up a wide-reaching spy ring within the Confederate capital and some say within the Confederate White House itself.

Van Lew began visiting Richmond's Libby Prison, where Union prisoners of war were imprisoned. As a humanitarian gesture, Van Lew brought food, medicine and books to the prisoners. She came out with military information. Newly arrived Union prisoners secretly recounted the strength and dispositions of Confederate troops they had seen on their way from the front to Richmond. As the war progressed, Van Lew was able to place fellow Union sympathizers within the Confederate War and Navy Departments and regularly smuggled messages out of Richmond in hollow eggs. General Grant would later say of her efforts, "You have sent me the most valuable information received from Richmond during the war."

Van Lew's most daring accomplishment remains shrouded in mystery and involved insinuating one of her former servants, Mary Elizabeth Bowser (also known as Mary Jane Richards), into the Confederate White House.

A spy is said to have infiltrated the White House of the Confederacy and passed on vital military information.

Bowser had been a slave of the Van Lew family, but Van Lew freed her and sent her north to be educated many years before the war. When Van Lew established her spy ring, she asked Bowser to return and work with her for the Union. Van Lew obtained a position for Bowser as a servant in the Confederate White House through the recommendation of a "friend" who provided supplies to that household.

Bowser pretended to be a bit "dull and unconcerned" but listened to and memorized conversations between Jefferson Davis and his visitors and the content of documents she was able to read while working in the house. Another Union spy, Thomas McNiven, noted that Bowser had a photographic memory and could report every word of the documents she saw. Jefferson Davis knew the Union somehow kept discovering Confederate plans but never discovered the leak in his own household.

Called the "White House," the Executive Mansion was rented from the City of Richmond by the Confederate government to serve as the residence of President Jefferson Davis and his family. The White House of the Confederacy is located at Clay and Twelfth Streets. Jefferson Davis; his wife, Varina; and their three small children moved into the White House in August 1861. Two more children were born in the White House, in 1861 and 1864, respectively. Five-year-old Joseph died from a fall at the house in 1864. Security was lax by modern standards. The president's two personal secretaries were armed. Additionally, a soldier was stationed at the front door and another at the basement door. Twelve soldiers were stationed on the grounds.

When the Union army captured Richmond in April 1865, Elizabeth Van Lew was the first person to raise the U.S. flag in the city. After the war, she insisted, "I'm not a Yankee," maintaining that she was only a good southerner holding to an old Virginia tradition of opposition to human bondage.

After the fall of Richmond, President Lincoln and his son Tad went to view the ruined city. Lincoln went to the second floor of the Confederate White House and triumphantly sat at Jefferson Davis's desk. Thousands of former slaves assembled outside to catch a glimpse of Lincoln.

Stories about Bowser's spying activities appeared as early as May 1900 in Richmond newspapers. In a 1910 interview with Elizabeth Van Lew's niece, Bowser was revealed as being part of the spy ring. Jefferson Davis's wife, Varina, however, publicly denied that a Black female spy could have infiltrated the Confederate White House and denied any knowledge of such a person as Mary Elizabeth Bowser.

According to U.S. Army intelligence sources, specific details of Bowser's activities and precise knowledge of the information passed to General Grant are unknown. In the interest of their protection, all records of Van Lew and her agents were destroyed after the war.

Mary Elizabeth Bowser was inducted into the U.S. Army Intelligence Hall of Fame at Fort Huachuca, Arizona, on June 30, 1995. Her great-granddaughter McEva Bowser attended the ceremony and accepted the award for her Civil War ancestor.

WOMEN OFFICERS IN THE CONFEDERATE ARMY

Technologically, the American Civil War was the first "modern" war, but medically, it still had its roots in the Middle Ages. American physicians received minimal training before the Civil War and were poorly trained by modern standards and even by the standards of European medicine of the day. European doctors went to four-year medical schools and received laboratory training. In America, most doctors received their training by serving as apprentices in lieu of formal education. Younger doctors who had actually attended medical schools trained for two years or less and received virtually no laboratory instruction. Germ theory, antiseptic medical practices, advanced medical equipment and organized hospitalization systems were virtually unknown in America prior to the Civil War.

Initially, when all concerned thought the war would be short, the Confederacy employed a policy of furloughing wounded soldiers to return home for recovery. In response, Southern women organized volunteer groups such as the Ladies' Soldiers' Relief Society and the Association for the Relief of Maimed Soldiers. Some women set up their own private hospitals in homes and donated buildings. The women of these organizations provided proper medical care for wounded and ill soldiers.

In August 1861, the Confederate army began building new larger hospitals in several Southern cities, and the furloughing policy was gradually halted. The growing number of hospitals undercut the need for women nurses in the South. In fact, female nursing was largely a Union, and not a Confederate,

Dr. Owen banned all women from his military hospitals, stating, "No more women or flies are to be admitted."

phenomenon. Nine thousand women served as nurses in Union hospitals, compared to only one thousand in Confederate hospitals, primarily because of the use of male slaves as nurses in the South. For example, Chimborazo Hospital in Richmond, Virginia, the largest Confederate hospital, with over five thousand beds in 150 buildings and tents, relied on male slaves rented from local plantation owners to serve as nurses.

In the mid-nineteenth century, sex discrimination prevented women from pursuing medicine, and those few who did were often obstructed by their male colleagues. The University of Pennsylvania established the first medical school in the country and set the pattern of barring women from obtaining medical degrees. It was not until January 23, 1849, that Elizabeth Blackwell became the first woman to receive a medical degree in America.

Not all women could be intimidated by conventional views. Although not a doctor, Lucy Mina Otey made a major contribution to Civil War– era medicine as a hospital administrator. At the outbreak of the Civil War, Lucy Mina Otey, a sixty-year-old widow, organized five hundred women of Lynchburg, Virginia, into the Ladies' Relief Society. The duties of the members of the society included preparing and delivering food to the wounded in hospitals, making bandages, mending clothes and assisting surgeons in any way possible. Women would write letters for soldiers and keep patients comfortable. One morning when arriving at a hospital, Mina Otey was denied access by order of Dr. W.O. Owen, the head of Lynchburg military hospitals. Dr. Owen ordered the removal of Otey and all women from the hospitals, stating, "No more women or flies are to be admitted."

Otey immediately traveled to Richmond to talk to President Jefferson Davis to get his personal permission to found her own hospital, run entirely by female nurses. Davis agreed. Corruption and mismanagement became a frequent issue in Confederate hospitals. The Confederate government eventually ordered the shutdown of all medical institutions that were not under direct government control. If a hospital was not headed by a commissioned officer who was at least a captain, then patients had to be moved. Because of the excellence of her hospital and her service to the Confederacy, Otey was named a captain in the Confederate army by President Jefferson Davis. Only one other woman received a commission in the Confederate army: Sally Tompkins, who ran a hospital in Richmond, Virginia.

Twenty-seven-year-old Sally Louisa Tompkins responded to the medical crisis brought on by the First Battle of Manassas by founding a private hospital in Richmond, Virginia, to care for the flood of Confederate wounded. Judge John Robertson had taken his family to the countryside for safety and left his home to Tompkins to use as a hospital. Tompkins supported the hospital from her ample private fortune.

When regulations were instituted requiring military hospitals be placed under military command, Tompkins petitioned President Jefferson Davis for an exception to the new rule. Instead, President Davis commissioned Tompkins a captain of cavalry, unassigned, making Robertson Hospital an official government facility. Captain Tompkins refused payment for her services. Of her military commission, dated September 9, 1861, she wrote, "I accepted the commission as Captain in the C.S.A. when it was offered. But, I would not allow my name to be placed upon the pay roll of the army."

Running a hospital presented many challenges, none more challenging than obtaining supplies. When the Civil War began, the Federal government cut off sales of medical supplies to the Confederacy. A Union naval blockade prevented ships from entering or leaving Southern ports. Unable to import enough medical supplies, the South began manufacturing medicines from its own native plants. Nine pharmaceutical laboratories were opened, including two in North Carolina, in Charlotte and Lincolnton. The Lincolnton lab grew poppies for opium and collected medicinal plants from all parts of the state. Citizens supported the war effort by providing both plants and bottles for medicines. When the Federal blockade tightened along the coast, Richmond faced riots in the streets. When supplies were difficult to get within the city, the Robertson Hospital hired a blockade runner to bring in surgical tools and medicines from Europe.

When Richmond was evacuated in April 1865, Tompkins and a number of volunteers remained at the hospital to treat the last of the patients. The Robertson Hospital discharged its last patient on June 13, 1865. During its four-year existence, Robertson Hospital treated 1,334 wounded soldiers with only 73 deaths, the lowest mortality rate of any military hospital operating during the Civil War.

UNSOLVED MYSTERIES

A MURDER AT BIZARRE

The strange case of Richard Randolph involved possibly one or two murders. In December 1789, twenty-one-year-old Richard Randolph, a young planter from one of the wealthiest and most powerful families in the state of Virginia, married his distant cousin, the "plain, pious and serious" seventeen-year-old Judith. In the fall of 1790, the newlyweds set up housekeeping at their new plantation home called Bizarre. For some time, all went well until Judith's attractive, lively sixteen-year-old sister known as Nancy moved into the house. Nancy had been having difficulty living under the same roof with her new stepmother and begged Judith for refuge. Visiting relatives soon commented on how fond Richard and Nancy were of each other. Some stumbled on them in each other's arms kissing. One frequent visitor, Mrs. Carter Paige, overheard Judith complaining of the intimacy between her husband and sister. Gossips soon began to say that Nancy was pregnant. The curious Mrs. Paige began spying on Nancy and soon discovered by peeping through a keyhole that when fully undressed, Nancy was clearly pregnant.

On Monday, October 1, 1792, Richard, Judith and Nancy arrived for a house party at a plantation called Glenlyvar in southern Virginia, the home of a cousin named Randolph Harrison. Nancy was wrapped in a thick cape and was so ill that she had to go immediately to bed.

Strange things happened that night. Randolph Harrison and his wife, Mary, later testified that they were awakened by screams coming from Nancy's bedroom. A servant soon came knocking at their bedroom door to tell them that Nancy was ill and to ask Mrs. Harrison to take her some laudanum. Mary Harrison went upstairs. Nancy's room could only be accessed by going through the bedroom occupied by Richard and Judith. As Mary Harrison entered the room, she saw Judith sitting up in bed, but Richard was in Nancy's room. The door to Nancy's room was bolted from the inside, but Richard opened the door when Mary Harrison knocked. Richard instructed her to put out her candle, which she did. Mary Harrison administered the laudanum and sat with Nancy in the dark for a few minutes before returning to her own room. Later that night, the Harrisons testified, they heard Richard going down the stairs and then returning after some time. The next day, Mary Harrison found bloodstains on the stairs.

The next day, Nancy remained in bed, wrapped in blankets. The Harrisons were told that Nancy suffered from recurring hysterical fits and had to be given laudanum to quiet her. At the end of the week, the house party ended, and Richard, Judith and Nancy returned home to Bizarre. At this point, a slave known as Old Esau went to his master, Randolph Harrison, and told him that he had seen the fetus of a white child being carried out into the yard.

Rumors began to fly that Richard and Nancy had birthed a child together and then murdered it. At first, Richard Randolph tried to ignore the rumors, but the clamor did not subside. Richard consulted with powerful friends and family members, admitting, "My character has lately been the subject of much conversation, blackened at the imputation of crimes at which humanity revolts." Richard retained an eighteenth-century legal "dream team" including Patrick Henry and John Marshall, future chief justice of the Supreme Court, and was advised to go on the offensive. Richard publicly announced that he would appear on April 1, 1793, before the Cumberland County Court to answer any charges placed against him. The case went to court. Witnesses testified for and against Richard and Nancy. The testimony of the slave Old Esau was never heard since a slave could not testify against a white person.

One of the witnesses called was Patsy Jefferson Randolph, daughter of Thomas Jefferson. She testified that Judith had once asked her if she knew of a remedy for Nancy's "colic." She had told Judith that gum guaiacum was an "excellent remedy" but warned that it was dangerous if taken in too great a quantity by someone who was pregnant because it could cause a miscarriage. After providing the proper warning, she had sent Nancy the remedy.

Patrick Henry questioned Judith on behalf of the defense. Judith swore that her husband, Richard, did not go downstairs that night for any reason. She was certain, she told the court, that he slept "by her side, although she could not sleep at all."

Ultimately, the court found Richard and Nancy not guilty of murder. While Nancy may have had a miscarriage, there was insufficient evidence to demonstrate that a murder had occurred. After the trial, Richard, Judith, Nancy and the women's brother, John Randolph, all returned to Bizarre to resume normal life. After the embarrassment of the trial, Nancy's activities were greatly curtailed. Judith closely watched her sister and husband and swore that Nancy must "be taught to expiate her sin" and that she must "earn her living and keep her place." Nancy now lived very much as a poor relation, almost as a servant.

Three years later, in 1796, Richard died. Judith was later to accuse Nancy of poisoning him. Once again, the wagging tongues wagged, doubting that it was Nancy who had poisoned Richard and suggesting that it was, in fact, Judith who tricked Nancy into administering a fatal concoction. Some said Judith, while doctoring her husband, changed the recipe for his medicine, instructing her sister Nancy to mix ingredients for a medicine that would surely kill the man. Richard took the medicine and writhed in agony for two days until he finally died. No one was ever brought to trial for the death of Richard Randolph, and whether he died of natural or unnatural causes remains a mystery.

THE BEALE TREASURE

For more than 160 years, people have been trying to find Virginia's most famous hidden fortune, the Beale Treasure. In an excavation six feet deep "in the county of Bedford about four miles from Buford's" lies 2,921 pounds of gold, 5,100 pounds of silver and some $200,000 worth of jewels.

Thomas Jefferson Beale came from a distinguished family. In 1668, King Charles II recommended one of Beale's ancestors for appointment as commander of Point Comfort, at the entrance of Norfolk Harbor. Beale himself was about six feet tall, with jet black hair and a swarthy complexion. He was a rugged outdoorsman, respected by men and "favored by the ladies."

In April 1817, Beale and a company of thirty individuals fond of adventure set out for the Great Western Plains to hunt buffaloes and grizzly bears. The party stopped in the small trading town of St. Louis to purchase the necessary outfits, procure a guide and obtain necessary information. The party left St. Louis on May 19 with the idea of a two-year expedition. The immediate goal was Santa Fe, which they reached in December. Nothing of interest occurred during the winter months, and the adventurers soon became heartily tired of the little Mexican town. In March, the band set out again following an immense herd of buffaloes. The party encamped in a ravine some 250 or 300 miles north of Santa Fe. In the light of the campfire, something sparkled in a cleft of the rocks. That something was gold.

For eighteen months, Beale and the others mined quantities of gold and silver. By the summer of 1819, the question of transferring the growing hoard to a more secure place was becoming critical. It was finally decided to send the treasure, in the care of Beale and ten others, to be buried in a cave in Bedford County near Buford's Tavern. All of the company had visited the cave, and it was considered a perfectly safe depository.

Beale and his friends stopped at Buford's Tavern for a month under the pretense of hunting. They visited the cave but found it unfit because it was too often visited by neighboring farmers who used it as a storage point for their sweet potatoes and other vegetables. They soon selected a better place. Beale returned west and found work still progressing favorably. Once again, he loaded up false-bottomed wagons and set out for Virginia, depositing yet another quantity of gold and silver with the original shipment.

Before leaving for Virginia the first time, Beale's companions on the plains became concerned that in the event of disaster overtaking the party, the buried treasure would be lost to their relatives. It was suggested that a reliable person in Virginia be selected who would be confided in to divide up the shares in the event of an unforeseen calamity.

Beale selected Robert Morriss, a tavern keeper for whose integrity he had great respect, to be a custodian of a locked box containing instructions on the disposition of the treasure. The box was left with Morriss in the spring of 1822, with instructions asking Morriss not to open it unless he had not heard from Beale in ten years. Beale was never heard from again after 1822. Morriss forgot about the box and, in fact, did not open it until 1845, some twenty-three years after it came into his possession. He found two letters to himself, some old receipts and some "unintelligible papers, covered with figures." These turned out to be three of the most puzzling cryptograms of all time.

The letters told the story of the discovery of the gold and directed Morriss to divide the treasure into thirty-one equal parts—one part for himself and one for the next of kin of each of the thirty members of the expedition. The undecipherable cryptograms supposedly gave the names of the next of kin and the location of the treasure. The cipher marked "No. 1" supposedly described the location of the vault where the treasure was buried, the one marked "No. 2" indicated the contents of the vault and "No. 3" stated the names and addresses of the next of kin of the expedition.

In a letter dated May 9, 1822, from St. Louis, Beale reassured Morriss that he would be sent a key to the ciphers: "Such a key I have left in the hands of a friend in this place, sealed, addressed to yourself, and endorsed 'Not to be delivered until June, 1832.'" The key never arrived. Morriss struggled vainly over the ciphers for the next seventeen years.

In 1862, Morriss shared the secret of the puzzling cryptograms, handing over the Beale papers to James B. Ward. Ward was a young man in comfortable financial circumstances who was ready to agree to the conditions laid down by Morriss for receipt of the trust. Ward agreed to devote as much time as practicable to the papers and, if successful in deciphering their meaning, to appropriate one-half of a share as a remuneration, the other half to be distributed to certain of Morriss's relatives and the remainder to be held in trust for the benefit of any claimants who might appear and be able to authenticate their claims. This latter amount was to be left intact for twenty years, and if still unclaimed, it would then revert to Ward.

Ward worked relentlessly on the codes until he finally broke cipher No. 2 by using a key based on the Declaration of Independence. The message reads:

> *I have deposited in the County of Bedford about four miles from Buford's* [present-day Montvale] *in an excavation or vault six feet below the surface of the ground the following articles belonging jointly to the parties whose names are given in number three herewith. The first deposit consisted of ten hundred and fourteen pounds of gold and thirty eight hundred and twelve pounds of silver deposited Nov. eighteen nineteen. The second was made Dec. eighteen twenty one and consisted of nineteen hundred and seven pounds of gold and twelve hundred and eighty eight of silver, also jewels obtained in St. Louis in exchange to save transportation and valued at thirteen thousand dollars. The above is securely packed in iron pots with iron covers. The vault is roughly lined with stone and the vessels rest on solid stone and are covered with others. Paper number one describes the exact locality of the vault so that no difficulty will be had in finding it.*

Ward became addicted to the quest and struggled with cipher Nos. 1 and 3 without luck for years, to the detriment of his family and fortune. "In consequence of the time lost in the above investigation I have been reduced from comparative affluence to absolute penury, entailing suffering upon those it was my duty to protect; and this, too, in spite of their remonstrance."

In 1885, Ward gave up and published *The Beale Papers*, which included Beale's letters and Morriss's testimony, as well as the record of his own efforts. Even in this undertaking, Ward was plagued by bad luck. All but a few copies of the pamphlet were destroyed by fire in the printing plant before distribution. Ward issued a stark warning to future hunters: "Devote only such time as can be spared from your legitimate business to the task, and if you can spare no time, let the matter alone."

The search for the Beale Treasure was next taken up by George and Clayton Hart of Roanoke, Virginia. In the summer of 1897, Clayton Hart, then a stenographer in the office of the auditor of the Norfolk and Western Railroad, was requested by N.H. Hazlewood, the chief clerk to the auditor, to make several copies of eight sheets of notepaper: two sheets simply headed "No. 1," three sheets headed "No. 2" and three sheets headed "No. 3."

Clayton asked Hazlewood about the strange papers. Hazlewood told him that they were connected to a treasure said to have been buried eighty years before near the foot of the Peaks of Otter, which overlooked his residence. Clayton obtained permission to retain a copy of the three ciphers.

Clayton Hart immediately began studying the meaningless figures. Some months later, he became aware that a man named Ward had spent many years trying to crack the ciphers. Clayton secured a copy of Ward's pamphlet and visited Ward in 1903.

From 1897 until 1907, Clayton Hart and his brother George spent practically every spare moment in an effort to find a key to the two unsolved ciphers. Separately and jointly, they turned to the Constitution, Shakespeare, the Declaration of Independence and numerous other books. Like Ward before them, they were unsuccessful in unraveling the mystery.

The Harts even turned to a medium. During a séance, the medium claimed he could lead the Harts to the treasure. Clayton and George decided to put the medium to the test. One spring evening in 1899, the Harts, with the medium in tow, left Roanoke about 5:00 p.m. in the family buggy. They carried picks, shovels, lanterns, ropes and axes—all the tools necessary to unearth treasure. Darkness settled over the land. Few people were moving about. The faint light of the receding moon offered just enough light to see objects of any size.

They drove across the railroad track, in the direction of the Peaks of Otter, stopping about a mile up Goose Creek. About four miles up Goose Creek, the medium stopped, took his bearings and then climbed a rail fence, jumped across a spring branch, ascended a hill and walked over the top and down into a crater-like place. Halting by the side of a large oak tree, the medium cried out, "There's the treasure."

The Harts began to dig. After six hours, they had succeeded in digging a hole approximately six feet deep and slightly larger than a grave. A few more inches down, Clayton Hart's pick struck a rock that produced a hollow sound, but the hoped-for pots of gold and silver were not underneath it.

The medium was again hypnotized and asked to reveal the whereabouts of the treasure. The medium pointed about two feet left of the hole that had been dug, directly underneath the great oak tree, and exclaimed, "There it is! You got over too far. Can't you see it?"

Crestfallen, the Harts went home. Several weeks later, however, Clayton returned to the spot alone. He went with dynamite and blasted out the old tree and about everything near it, but there were still no pots of gold, silver and jewels.

The Harts continued their efforts off and on over fifty years, finally publishing in 1964 an account of the treasure and the efforts to find it.

In 1966, about one hundred computer experts and cryptographers formed the Beale Cipher Association in an attempt to outwit Thomas Jefferson Beale. Even this prestigious group has so far been thwarted. While still unable to crack Beale's codes, the Beale Cipher Association has demonstrated through running the ciphers through computers that the codes are not just random numbers. There is definitely a message contained in ciphers No. 1 and No. 3. The Beale ciphers have been identified as multiple substitution ciphers. Since every letter in the cipher is represented by several different numbers, it is one of the most difficult ciphers to break.

It was not unusual for an educated man like Beale to be expert in cryptography. In those early days, waylaying other people's messages was common practice. To protect their secrets, people created ciphers based on common books of the day. Thirty years before Beale began his odyssey, Thomas Jefferson invented a cipher wheel (a coding machine) that was so devilishly clever that a similar device was used by American military intelligence in World War II.

The search for the treasure goes on. In 1983, a Pennsylvania woman spent almost two months in jail for digging up a church graveyard in search of the treasure. A recent solution gave instructions to penetrate a deep-water pit in a disused mine on Purgatory Stream, forty-five miles northeast of Roanoke. The hunting party found nothing more than a ninety-pound hunk of colonial-era pig iron. Another treasure hunter, having located a likely site, fenced off the area, hired guards and brought in a bulldozer. He found the remains of a 1930s car.

Many people fervently believe in the existence of the Beale Treasure. Others do not, producing mountains of circumstantial evidence to expose the Beale Treasure as a hoax. The most damning evidence, of course, is that the original letters written by Thomas Jefferson Beale cannot be produced. Researcher Louis Kruh raised further doubts in the journal

Cryptologia, citing stylometric evidence that indicates that James Ward's pamphlets and the letters supposedly written by Thomas Beale were written by one and the same person. Another researcher, Richard H. Greaves, who studied the legend for twenty-five years, concluded that the playwright John W. Sherman, owner of a newspaper called the *Lynchburg Virginian*, was the author of the Beale Papers. According to this theory, Sherman (a relative of James Ward's) regarded the Beale Treasure story like the other thrilling "dime novels" then popular about the daring and outrageous deeds of Wyatt Earp, Annie Oakley and other larger-than-life figures. Originally written in aid of the families of victims of a major Lynchburg fire and put on sale for $0.50 (approximately $13.00 today) in 1885, the novelette was resurrected in 1886 and advertised intensively at $0.10 per copy (approximately $2.50) as Sherman's newspaper floundered financially. According to Greaves, the pamphlet was advertised in the *Lynchburg Virginian* eighty-four times over five months to generate income for the newspaper. Lynchburg had a population of twenty-two thousand in 1885, and the newspaper had a circulation of sixteen thousand. Despite all of the alleged public interest in the treasure, the other Lynchburg newspaper, the *Daily News*, only mentioned the booklet once, when it was originally released. Apparently, residents of Lynchburg had their doubts about the treasure in 1885. The novelette failed to save Sherman from financial ruin but lived on to become the centerpiece of one of the most enduring treasure legends in Virginia.

THE STRANGE CASE
OF EDGAR ALLAN POE

Each spring, the Mystery Writers of America present the Edgar Awards, the most prestigious award a mystery writer can receive. This award is, fittingly, named after Edgar Allan Poe, the father of the modern detective story ("The Murders in the Rue Morgue," "The Gold Bug"). It is even more fitting that Poe's untimely death remains one of history's great unsolved mysteries.

Poe was born in Boston in 1809 but was orphaned at an early age. A Richmond couple became his foster parents, and Poe spent his youth in Richmond, finally going off to college at the University of Virginia. Young Poe, now eighteen, incurred gambling debts and quarreled with his foster father. He dropped out of the University of Virginia and joined the United States Army under an assumed name. This didn't work out either. In 1829, Edgar Allan Poe announced that he would make his way in the world by becoming a poet and writer. Poe became the first American writer to earn a living (a very modest living) through writing alone.

On September 27, 1849, Edgar Allan Poe left Richmond bound for Philadelphia, where he had been commissioned to edit a collection of poems. Poe may never have made it to Philadelphia, and he definitely did not make it to New York to escort his aunt back to Richmond for his impending wedding. On October 3, 1849, one Joseph Walker, an employee of the *Baltimore Sun*, found Poe lying in a Baltimore gutter. Poe was never to leave Baltimore. The Poe Museum in Richmond, the repository of many of Poe's greatest literary works, tells us that the writer was found "semiconscious and dressed in cheap,

Many theories have been put forward to explain the mysterious death of Edgar Allan Poe.

ill-fitting clothes so unlike Poe's usual mode of dress that many believe that Poe's own clothing had been stolen." Edgar Allan Poe remained incoherent, gripped by delirium and hallucinations, unable to explain how he had come to be found in Baltimore, senseless on the streets, in dirty clothes not his own. Poe died on the night of October 7, 1849, calling out for "Reynolds." The identity of the mysterious Reynolds remains unknown.

For over 150 years, people have speculated on the cause of Poe's death. Numerous theories have been put forward, including: he died of a beating (1857), he died of epilepsy (1875), he drank himself to death (1921), he died of heart disease (1926), he died of toxic poisoning (1970), he died of diabetes (1977), he died of hypoglycemia (1979), he died of rabies (1996) and he was murdered (1998). Other theories proclaim he died of a brain tumor, from heavy metal poisoning or from the flu.

The most popular theory is that Poe died as a result of a practice called "cooping." Cooping was a form of voter fraud practiced in the nineteenth century. Innocent people were snatched off the streets and imprisoned in a room called "the coop," where they were fed drugs and alcohol to gain their silence and complicity in a scheme whereby they would vote multiple times in the same election. The uncooperative would be beaten into submission. Sometimes they were killed. Election fraud is a high-stakes game. The now compliant victims were forced to change clothes between casting votes and were often forced to wear wigs and fake beards so that election officials would not recognize them at the polls.

There is circumstantial evidence that indicates that Poe may have run afoul of such a scheme. Baltimore elections were notoriously violent and corrupt in 1840. An election for sheriff was going on at the time. Poe was found on the street on Election Day near Ryan's Fourth Ward polls, which was both a bar and a place where votes were cast. Is it possible that Edgar Allan Poe was kidnapped, drugged and beaten to death in a voter fraud conspiracy? Perhaps, but the theory still doesn't explain how Poe got the one hundred miles from Philadelphia to Baltimore. Surely, it would have been easier for the conspirators to pluck someone off the streets of Baltimore itself.

Another theory, put forth by writer John E. Walsh in 2000, suggests a more personal reason for Poe's predicament, one that involved a lady. Sarah Royster was the teenage sweetheart of Edgar Allan Poe. Sarah's father did not approve of Poe and put an end to the relationship while Poe was at the University of Virginia. Sarah married a very wealthy man named Alexander Shelton and enjoyed a happy marriage until Shelton's death in 1844. In 1848, Edgar Allan Poe came back into Sarah's life. Sarah attended Poe's lectures in Richmond, and by September 1849, the couple was thought to have had an understanding and was on the verge of marriage. Once again, Sarah's family did not approve, perhaps thinking that Poe was a fortune hunter. John Walsh argues that Poe was in Philadelphia when he was confronted by Sarah's three brothers, who roughly warned him against trying to marry their sister. A frightened Poe, wanting no further encounters with the brothers, disguised himself (this accounts for the shoddy wardrobe in which Poe was found) and headed back to Richmond to marry Sarah. The brothers intercepted Poe in Baltimore, savagely beat him and left him in the gutter. He subsequently died. Possible? Perhaps, but we may never know the truth.

Edgar Allan Poe was buried in Baltimore. An imposing grave monument was dedicated to Poe on November 17, 1875. Beginning in January 1949 and continuing until January 19, 2009 (the 200th anniversary of Poe's birth), a still unidentified stranger entered the cemetery on the night of January 19 and left a partial bottle of cognac and three roses on Poe's grave. Who was the "Poe Toaster"? Yet another unsolved mystery.

THE BRUTON PARISH MYSTERY

There exists a cache of hidden documents, the contents of which are so powerful that their release could forever change the course of world civilization. For centuries, these documents have been protected by a secret society known as the Order of the Illumined, or the Illuminati. These documents have been deemed so critical to mankind's future that they have been called the Seventh Seal. Interestingly, these keys to the future of mankind are buried in the cemetery of the Bruton Parish Episcopal Church in Colonial Williamsburg. The Seventh Seal cache is said to be housed in a brick vault constructed by Sir Francis Bacon (1561–1626), a favorite courtier of Queen Elizabeth I. Apparently, some of Bacon's papers were also left behind in the vault, including documentation proving his authorship of the Shakespearian plays; his original Tudor birth records showing him to be the illegitimate son of Queen Elizabeth I; an unabridged version of the King James Version of the Bible, translated by Bacon; and more—including gold!

On September 9, 1991, a group of New Age mystics did an unauthorized dig for the Bruton vault in the dark hours of the night. Their intention was to follow up on a dig performed in 1938 that uncovered the church's original foundations and to bring to the public's attention knowledge of the precious hidden national treasure buried at Bruton Parish. Church elders were not happy with the midnight digging, and by court order, the New Age seekers were forbidden from returning to Virginia.

In an attempt to put an end to this urban legend, Bruton Parish followed up on the midnight dig by commissioning archaeologists, including Colonial Williamsburg archaeologist Marley Brown, to retrace the steps of the 1938

Does the cemetery of the Bruton Parish Church conceal powerful knowledge that could change the course of world civilization?

excavation to answer a question that arose in 1985. In 1985, surface tests using radar-like equipment indicated that there was something under the Bruton Parish cemetery different from untouched soil. That something could be the hidden vault, a tree root or surface dirt used to fill in the 1938 excavation.

After seven days of once again uncovering the remains of the original church walls, workers looking for Sir Francis Bacon's vault dug about nine feet deep and reportedly found an object with brass tacks in it. Church officials said it was a casket and would not allow them to dig further. By August 1992, the archaeologists hired by the parish concluded that there was no hidden vault. End of story.

But this is a story that will never end because of the way it began. New Age followers claim the 1992 church-sponsored dig was bogus. The parish knowingly dug in the wrong places. There may also be sinister forces at work to suppress the release of the great secret, according to some conspiracy theorists. These sinister forces may include the Skull and Bones secret society at Yale University (of which George W. Bush is a member), as well as Colonial Williamsburg's benefactor, the Rockefeller family.

So just how did this legend get started in the first place? There was, of course, a Sir Francis Bacon. Bacon was a well-known English philosopher, statesman and scientist. Bacon is regarded as the father of empiricism and the modern "scientific method." Bacon's movement for the advancement of learning was connected with the German Rosicrucian movement. The Rosicrucians were and are a secret society built on esoteric truths of the ancient past, which, concealed from the average man, provide insight into nature, the physical universe and the spiritual realm. Bacon's book *New Atlantis* portrays a land ruled by Rosicrucians. How did Francis Bacon, the Renaissance intellectual, become the centerpiece of an urban legend? Enter one Manly Palmer Hall.

A junior high school dropout from a broken home, Manly Palmer Hall, who had a photographic memory, became a one-stop scholar of ancient ideas. In 1920, at the age of nineteen, the charismatic and movie-star handsome Hall was running a church in Los Angeles. He delivered Sunday lectures about Rosicrucianism and Theosophy, the mystical philosophical system founded by Madame Helena Blavatsky, as well as other esoteric teachings. Alternative religious movements were busting out all over Southern California in the first half of the twentieth century, and the devastatingly handsome Manly Palmer Hall attracted many rich female followers, which allowed him to produce his masterwork, *The Secret Teachings of All Ages*. Through his writings and endless lecturing, Manly Palmer Hall became one of the people principally responsible for the birth of the New Age religious movement in the United States, first in California, starting in the 1920s and then beyond.

Manly Palmer Hall and his second wife, Marie Bauer Hall (they were married in 1950), are the source of the Bruton Parish mystery. While acting as a volunteer at Hall's church in the 1930s, the then Marie Bauer struck up a conversation with a visitor waiting to see Hall. The visitor was a scholar who claimed to have deciphered codes hidden in Shakespeare's plays that told of a treasure hidden by Sir Francis Bacon under a church in Virginia. Marie Bauer, who said she was clairvoyant, felt an immediate connection between the lost treasure described by the visitor and Bruton Parish Church. Bauer had once been given a tea towel from Williamsburg that included a picture of Bruton Parish Church.

Marie took her finding to Manly Hall, and together they spent many happy hours deciphering hidden codes placed in various writings contemporary to Francis Bacon, including *A Collection of Emblems* (George Wither, 1635) and various Shakespearean plays, which demonstrated, at least to them, that a ten-foot-by-ten-foot brick vault was buried twenty feet deep at the Bruton

Parish Church, its exact location marked by certain strategically placed encoded memorials in the church cemetery. In 1938, Marie Bauer initiated the excavation that revealed the foundations of the original Bruton Church but no hidden vault. Marie would have been happy to continue digging up the church graveyard, but further excavation was halted by church officials.

For some, the exact location of the Bruton Parish vault remains an unsolved mystery.

UFOs

O n March 23, 2005, during a thunderstorm, a Clifton woman observed something very strange, very strange indeed. The woman's husband reported:

We had a power outage last night and my wife was awakened by the answering machine clicking on and off as the power tried to recover, and then it went out completely. She went to the front door to see if it was raining or windy and saw a very large object hovering over a nearby house about 1/8 of a mile from our house. It was larger than the house, seemed to be at an angle to her view with the bottom exposed and had lights all around it evenly spaced. When it began to move away, several lightning flashes were seen and then it was gone. The power returned two hours later.

The appearance lasted just a few seconds, from the "balls of light" formation to the vertical lightning flash. The woman may have witnessed a natural "Rare Atmospheric Phenomenon" involving multiple ball lightning. Alternatively, she may have seen a UFO.

Virginia is no stranger to UFO sightings, but the best documented and most controversial sightings occurred in 1952 during the so-called Washington Flap. From July 19 to July 29, 1952, a series of UFO sightings over Northern Virginia and the city of Washington electrified the country and prompted President Harry S. Truman to call the U.S. Air Force for explanations. At 11:40 p.m. on Saturday, July 19, an air traffic controller

The Pentagon brass tried to explain away numerous UFO sightings, but not everyone was convinced.

at Washington National Airport spotted seven objects on radar. No known aircraft were in the area, and the objects were not following any established flight paths. This was highly irregular. The equipment was checked and found to be in perfect order. When the objects moved into prohibited air space over the White House and U.S. Capitol, the air traffic controller called Andrews Air Force Base.

The air traffic controllers at Andrews reported that they had no unusual objects on their radar screens, but an airman soon called the base's control tower to report the sighting of a strange object. Airman William Brady saw an "object which appeared to be like an orange ball of fire, trailing a tail....[It was] unlike anything I had ever seen before." At 12:30 a.m. on July 20, another person in the National Airport control tower reported seeing "an orange disk at about 3,000 feet altitude." At 3:00 a.m., shortly before two jet fighters from Newcastle Air Force Base in Delaware arrived over Washington, all of the objects vanished from the radar at National Airport. However, when the jets ran low on fuel and left, the objects returned.

There were also witnesses. Joseph Gigandet of Alexandria, sitting on the front porch of his home, claimed to see "a red cigar-shaped object" that sailed slowly over his house just prior to the radar sightings at National Airport.

On July 22, the *Washington Post* broke the story. "The Air Force disclosed last night it has received reports of an eerie visitation by unidentified aerial objects—perhaps a new type of 'flying saucer'—over the vicinity of the Nation's Capital. For the first time, so far as known, the objects were picked up by radar—indicating actual substance rather than mere light."

The article went on to report, "The airport traffic control center said Capital-National Airlines Flight 610, reported observing a light following it from Herndon, Va. about 20 airline miles from Washington, to within four miles of National Airport."

On July 28, 1952, the headlines of the *Alexandria Gazette* read, "Jet Fighters Outdistanced by 'Flying Saucers' over Mt. Vernon and Potomac." The article went on to explain:

> *Jet fighters of the Eastern Interceptor Command today were maintaining a 24-hour alert for "flying saucers" over the Alexandria vicinity. The order was issued after radar operators at the CAA Air Route Traffic Control Center at National Airport sighted the mysterious objects Saturday night—the second time in eight days. The Air Force said two jets pursued "between four and twelve" of the elusive objects Saturday night, but the pilots reported they were unable to get any closer than seven miles before the saucers disappeared. One pilot said he saw "a steady white light" about ten miles east of Mt. Vernon. His supersonic jet, traveling at a speed of more than 600 miles per hour, was outdistanced when he sought to overtake the object.*

The sightings of July 26–27 made headlines across the country and must have unnerved President Truman, who personally called the U.S. Air Force's UFO expert, Captain Ruppelt, and asked for an explanation of the sightings. Ruppelt told the president that the sightings might have been caused by temperature inversion, in which a layer of warm, moist air covers a layer of cool, dry air closer to the ground. This condition can cause radar signals to bend and give false returns.

On July 29, 1952, the *Alexandria Gazette* reported, "Saucers Seen Again Early This Morning: Flying Saucers Circled the Northern Virginia Area Again This Morning." The article went on to explain:

> *The CAA says its radar picked up the saucers about six straight hours early today as they circled between Herndon, and Andrews Field....Saucer experts from Wright Field, Ohio have been called to Washington for a special conference on the phenomenon. The group was scheduled to arrive last night, but was delayed by plane trouble and will instead meet today.*

On July 29, 1952, in the largest press conference held at the Pentagon since the conclusion of World War II, the air force declared the visual sightings over Washington as misidentified aerial phenomena. The air force also stated that the radar-visual reports could be explained by temperature inversion. Neither Captain Ruppelt, who left the air force, nor any of the radar and control tower personnel at Washington National Airport agreed with the air force explanation.

PARANORMAL TALES

VIRGINIA SUPERSTITIONS

Virginians have been developing superstitions for over almost five centuries. Some of these still have a noticeable following, particularly in the mountains of southwest Virginia. People in this area were cut off and therefore developed a keen interest in the pragmatic use of charms, potions, spells and signs—anything that could allow them to predict what was coming or allow them to change the course of events.

Many of these superstitions and folk remedies involve healing. In the realm of superstitious practices, these might involve, for example, curing a child with whooping cough by passing the child under the belly of a donkey nine times. Alternatively, you could cure the child by hanging an adder stone around the child's neck. The adder stone was said to draw out poison and illness.

Children were not the only ones to benefit from folk wisdom. An expectant mother could cut the pain of childbirth by putting scissors or an axe under her bed. Shoes and socks seem to have great medicinal value. If you turn your shoes upside down before going to bed, you won't get foot cramps. If you smell your socks before bed—first the right and then the left; the sequence is vital—you will never catch a cold. If you do manage to get a sore throat, tie a dirty sock around your neck. This will cure it.

There is just so much useful information out there. Tie an onion to your bed post to keep away colds (and probably people). If you carry a buckeye in your pocket, you will never be troubled with hemorrhoids. Worried about going bald? The sap of a grapevine will grow hair on a bald head.

Virginians have been developing superstitions for over almost five centuries. Some of these still have a noticeable following.

Many superstitions involve attracting good luck. Start off every New Year's Day by eating black-eyed peas. Each black-eyed pea you eat will ensure a day of good luck, so be sure to eat 365. If the first person who comes to your house on New Year's Day is a man, this guarantees that you will have good luck. If you make a wish on a new moon, it will come true. To ensure good luck in health and love, find a red ear of corn.

Many more superstitions involve avoiding bad luck. If a black cat crosses your path, make an X in the air three times to avoid bad luck. You must do this quickly. If a cat sits with its tail to the fire, it means bad luck is on the way. Similarly, if a rooster crows at a certain hour for three nights in a row, it means bad luck is on the way. Here are things that you must not do around the house. You must not sing before breakfast or you will be crying before supper. You must not put your left foot forward when leaving the house; bad luck will surely come. You must not sweep a house at night or bad luck will follow. Do your cleaning early; sweeping in the morning clears out the evil spirits.

When traveling, you will want to avoid bad luck. If you start a trip and forget something in the house, don't just grab it and run. Sit down before you start out again or you will have bad luck. When you leave a house, close the back door before you open the front door or you will have bad luck. If, when starting on a journey, the first living thing you meet is either a woman or cat, you will have bad luck.

Of course, the worst luck you could have would be to attract the attention of evil spirits. There were many wise pronouncements on how to avoid this. You should have two clocks in the house set at different times to confuse the devil. When harvesting apples, leave at least one apple on the tree to keep the devil away. If you spill salt, throw a pinch over your left shoulder to keep the devil away. If you forget and throw it over your right shoulder, you are not protected. If you are drinking spirits outside, pour some on the ground to satisfy ghostly spirits that might otherwise be offended.

In the event that you ignored all of the sage advice you had been given about avoiding bad luck and began to experience a run of bad luck, you could always break the cycle by pulling a pig's tail.

Superstitions continued to evolve, and during the nineteenth century, many superstitions grew up around the topics of love and marriage. To be "lucky in love," a woman must reject a suitor whose last name began with the same initial as her own. Hence the saying, "To change the name, but not the letter, is a change for the worse, and not the better." Here are other things to consider. If a woman carries an acorn in her pocket, she will be blessed with perpetual youth. If you are unmarried and sit at the corner of the table, you will not marry for seven years.

If a couple became engaged, all sorts of omens were considered for the wedding day. Wednesday was considered the luckiest day of the week to hold a wedding. Hence the saying, "Monday for wealth, Tuesday for health, Wednesday—the best day of all! Thursday for crosses, Friday for losses, Saturday—no luck at all." Wedding rehearsals were held in the nineteenth century, but it was considered bad luck for the bride to participate. A friend would take her place at the rehearsal. On the day of the wedding, a bride could bring on bad luck if she looked into a mirror after she was dressed for the ceremony. To avoid this, the clever girl left off a glove or a slipper before taking a final peek. Also, on the day of the wedding it was considered bad luck for the bride and groom to see each other prior to the ceremony. A good omen for the wedding day was a gray horse pulling the wedding carriage. Apparently, a horse of that color ensured a happy marriage.

BIGFOOT IN VIRGINIA

Is it possible that Bigfoot roams through the woods of Virginia? For generations, there have been sightings of Bigfoot-like creatures across America. The legend grew in popularity in 1967, when two men in California filmed a huge and hairy beast in the woods walking on two feet and at one point turning directly toward the camera. The clip is known as the "Patterson-Gimlin film," named for the men involved in its filming. Over the years, the film has been surrounded by controversy, with many experts concluding that the subject captured on film is non-human, while others have judged it "a man in an ape suit."

In Virginia, a man named Billy Willard runs the Sasquatch Watch of Virginia, a Bigfoot and wildlife scientific field research group. The group conducts field investigations and field research of reported encounters or habitual recurring encounters of Bigfoot in Virginia. Willard's group has identified thirty-eight counties in Virginia that have reported Bigfoot-like sightings.

This account from Spotsylvania County is typical of the type of sightings that the Sasquatch Watch of Virginia documents:

> *It was following a foxhunt and we were getting up hounds about the edge of dark. My husband, my granddaughter and I were on one side of the pond when suddenly I saw movement on the other side. I observed what appeared to be a 7 foot man in black walking slowly across the field towards the woods....I blinked to try to get a better focus while at the same time saying*

"what the hell is that?" About that time my husband and granddaughter caught sight of it and my husband swung the truck around to try to get closer. He said "is it a bear?" At this time the "thing" started running, and when I say running I mean RUNNING! I have never seen such a large animal/person be able to run so swiftly nor so gracefully! It was almost as if it "glided" across the ground. Upon realizing that a bear could never run like that on two legs we were baffled as to WHAT this "thing" is. I have never seen anything like it before and if someone asked me to describe it the best way I can I would have to say it looked like a gorilla but was taller but leaner and much more graceful and swift.

In 2009, a Bristol man claimed that he and a hunting companion encountered a Bigfoot-type beast near Gum Hill in Washington County. The two came across a large figure (now known as the Beast of Gum Hill) sitting on a rock. As the men approached, the figure rose, whistled and made other noises and then ran off. The witness described its face as "Neanderthal."

Tales of a Bigfoot-like creature in Virginia date back to the nineteenth century. An 1868 news article in the *Memphis Daily Avalanche* reported that the farm of Silas Brown of Independent Hill, in Prince William County,

For generations, there have been sightings of Bigfoot-like creatures across America.

was being visited by "an immense figure…with large horns and terrible claws." The creature was described as being three times as large as a man and having huge arms. The creature appeared numerous times around the farm, and at one point, Brown and a neighbor were attacked when the beast threw a huge rock at them.

A more recent encounter may have occurred in Fairfax County. On May 12, 1979, the front page of the *Washington Post* carried an article titled "The Mount Vernon Monster." For nine months, in 1978 and 1979, a strange creature wailed and screamed nightly in the woods just a mile from historic Mount Vernon, George Washington's estate in Virginia. Some people called it the "Mount Vernon Monster," others "Bigfoot." The creature was elusive, frustrating capture attempts by the police, flyovers by a U.S. Park police helicopter, searches by volunteer youth patrols and the determined efforts of the Fairfax County game warden to track it down.

Witnesses began to appear. One witness reported, "Just as I got to the edge of the woods, it screamed a second time. And I could feel the reverberations.…I could feel it in my chest, like if you stand in front of a bass speaker, I could feel it in my chest, and it made every hair on the back of my neck stand up. And I could hear twigs break and branches snapping."

Years later, accounts are still circulating:

> *I was one of those teenagers in the late '70s who heard the Mt. Vernon monster. I actually had a tape recording of it but my little sister taped over it. Yes, down an unpaved road leading to Union Farm we parked our cars late at night and quietly waited. Dogs would start barking nearby and sure enough we then heard the howl of the Mt. Vernon Monster. I also have a friend who saw the creature not far from the back gate of Mt. Vernon, off Old Mt. Vernon Road near the Potomac River one snowy day. She was nearly 200 yards away and at first glance thought it was a man walking towards the woods. She quickly realized it was not. She described it as large and hairy.*

The story made its way into oral history projects, which are now being cited by monster hunters as historical authentication of the creature's existence. "One of the game wardens said, 'The thing seems to know when you leave the woods, then it starts to holler.' One resident said she spotted the monster. She described it as a creature about six feet tall, which lumbered into the woods after being sighted."

The howling stopped as abruptly as it began, but the story lives on despite the fact that in 1999, researchers David Leeming and Jake Page claim to have unmasked the Mount Vernon Monster as a hoax. Sound recordings of the monster's roars were sent to Eugene Morton at the National Zoo for analysis. Morton, an expert in interpreting animal sounds, reported that the monster's howls were, in fact, the chirp of a baby robin played at one-eighth normal speed over stereo speakers, turning it into a hideous, low rumble.

MONSTERS UNMASKED

According to the legend of the Richmond Vampire, a blood-covered creature with jagged teeth and skin hanging from its body stalks Hollywood Cemetery in Richmond, Virginia. Hollywood Cemetery is a likely place to encounter a vampire. It is a large, sprawling, Victorian-era cemetery often called the Valhalla of the Confederacy since it is the final resting place of twenty-five Confederate generals (including George Pickett of "Pickett's Charge" and the dashing cavalry commander J.E.B. Stuart), as well as the only Confederate States president, Jefferson Davis.

The legend of the Richmond Vampire got started in 1925 after the collapse of the Church Hill Railway Tunnel. Apparently, the collapse outed a vampire. A blood-covered monster with jagged teeth and rotting, hanging skin emerged from the cave-in and raced toward Hollywood Cemetery. Pursued by an angry mob, the creature fled into the hillside mausoleum of one W.W. Pool. Curiously, the mausoleum of W.W. Pool has no birth date, just a death date: 1922, three years before the cave-in. The mob found no sign of the monster, which had vanished, and it presumably still haunts the cemetery. Certainly some people believe this, reporting sightings of paranormal orbs of light near the crypt to this day.

Researcher Gregory Maitland, however, is not a believer. Maitland discovered that the legend is based on the true story of the collapse of the Church Hill Tunnel, without the vampire. One living man emerged from the disaster that gobbled up a still unknown number of transient laborers. That man was twenty-eight-year-old railroad fireman Benjamin F. Mosby.

Hollywood Cemetery in Richmond is a likely place to encounter a vampire.

Mosby was horribly burned, several of his teeth were broken and layers of his skin were hanging hideously from his body as he emerged from the collapse. Mosby, in shock, headed toward the James River, in the general direction of Hollywood Cemetery. Concerned onlookers overtook him and took him to Grace Hospital, where he later died from his injuries. But the legend of the vampire lives on.

Another, far grislier urban legend relates to a homicidal maniac. According to this urban legend, "Bunny Man" murdered teenage couples at night and took their bodies to a railroad bridge near Fairfax Station, christened by local teenagers as "Bunny Man Bridge." The body count rises with each retelling of the story, having now reached thirty-two.

Some of the latest iterations of the Bunny Man legends say: (1) a young man from Clifton, Virginia, who came upon Bunny Man Bridge later killed his parents and dragged their bodies into the woods to hang them from the bridge and then killed himself; (2) in the 1940s, three teenagers were at the Bunny Man Bridge on Halloween night. The three youths were found dead, hanged from the bridge. Police discovered a note that read, "You'll never catch the Bunny Man!" and (3) in 2001, six local students searched the area. They found mutilated bunny parts during their search and left the forest after they heard noises and saw figures moving around in the woods.

One particularly lurid account is rich in historical details. In 1904, an asylum for the criminally insane located in Clifton, Virginia, was transporting inmates to a new facility when a road accident allowed ten dangerous lunatics to escape. All but two were recaptured, but Douglas J. Grifon and Marcus Wallster remained at large. Local inhabitants soon began finding the remains of skinned, half-eaten rabbits hanging from trees. Eventually, Wallster's body was discovered hanging from a remote railroad bridge near Clifton. Wallster was clutching a bloody hatchet. In the years that followed, dead rabbits continued to appear and murdered teenagers were found hanging from the same bridge.

Do these stories have any basis in fact? Was the Bunny Man real? Brian A. Conley, historian-archivist with the Fairfax County Public Library, undertook the task of tracking down the real Bunny Man. Conley discovered the origins of the legend in a *Washington Post* article of October 22, 1970: "Man in Bunny Suit Sought in Fairfax." According to the article, the real Bunny Man accosted a young couple on Guinea Road:

> *Air Force Academy Cadet Robert Bennett told police that shortly after midnight last Sunday he and his fiancée were sitting in a car in the 5400 block of Guinea Road when a man "dressed in a white suit with long bunny ears" ran from the nearby bushes and shouted: "You're on private property and I have your tag number."*

The man then threw a hatchet through the right front car window. No one was injured, and the man ran off into the woods. On October 31, the newspaper reported that the Bunny Man had reappeared: "A man wearing a furry rabbit suit with two long ears appeared—again—on Guinea Road in Fairfax County Thursday night, police reported, this time wielding an ax and chopping away at a roof support on a new house."

Confronted by a patrolling security guard, Bunny Man made his escape—but not before threatening the security guard. Conley ferreted out the official police report, which read, "At 10:30 p.m. on October 29, 1970 six officers responded to 5307 Guinea Road for 'a subject dressed as a rabbit with an ax.'" Bunny Man made one more documented appearance, accusing Kings Park West residents of dumping trash.

CIVIL WAR SPECTERS AND OTHER GHOSTS

D o ghosts from the American Civil War still walk among us, or are reported spectral visions and unearthly things that go bump in the night the product of overactive imaginations? Virginia experienced twenty-six major battles and four hundred smaller engagements on its soil during the course of the war, giving ample opportunity for the creation of disgruntled spirits among those who died in battle.

Bodies of dead and wounded men were hit over and over again until they simply fell apart and became unrecognizable remnants of bloody flesh rather than corpses. There were big charges and little charges, with bayonet fighting when the men came to close quarters, and at times Union and Confederate flags waved side by side on the parapets, with bullets shredding them into tattered streamers....Men fired at one another through chinks in the logs, or stabbed through the chinks with their bayonets, or reached over the top to swing clubbed muskets. Where the Vermont Brigade was fighting, men were seen to spring on top of the logs and fire down on their enemies as fast as their comrades could pass loaded muskets up to them. Each man would get off a few rounds before he was shot, and usually when one of these men fell someone else would clamber up to take his place. Dead men fell on top of wounded men, and unhurt men coming up to fight would step on the hideous writhing pile-up.

This is how historian Bruce Catton describes the fighting at Spotsylvania Court House in 1864 in his book *A Stillness at Appomattox*. This level of combat intensity was not unique to Spotsylvania, however. Similar scenes were played out at Manassas, Cold Harbor and hundreds of other Civil War battlefields large and small, giving rise to many stories of battlefield hauntings. It is not remarkable that such stories should exist. There is a huge body of circumstantial evidence of battlefield hauntings stretching back to ancient times, when ghosts were seen and heard to engage on the plains of Marathon after the battle (the Battle of Marathon was fought in 490 BC). In the 1930s, visitors to this region of Greece were still claiming to have heard the sound of metal clashes and screams coming from the battlefield. In *Vita Isiclori*, Damascius tells us that after a battle outside the walls of Rome against the Huns in AD 452, ghosts were reported to still be fighting for three days and nights after the battle, the clash of their weapons being heard all over the city. The first major battle of the English Civil War (1662) produced a well-documented case of ghost armies fighting as reliable witnesses reported the phantom soldiers engaged in battle. King Charles I was so intrigued by the stories that he sent a royal commission to investigate. The trusted officers of the commission reported back that they, too, had seen the ghastly spectacle and even recognized the ghosts of some of their fallen friends. The phenomenon continued for some time, gradually lessening over time, until now there are only occasional reports of people hearing the sounds of battle at Edgehill.

The Spotsylvania Battlefield is one place where the ghosts of Civil War soldiers appear. A fierce battle raged around Spotsylvania Court House on and off from May 8 through May 21, 1864. Over four thousand soldiers were killed. The Bloody Angle was the site of the longest, most savage hand-to-hand combat of the Civil War. In recent years, American Battlefield Ghost Hunters Society has investigated paranormal activity around the Bloody Angle, often sprinkling the area with pieces of beef jerky and chewing tobacco, which would have been luxuries at the time of the Civil War, to lure the spirits of dead soldiers to the spot. The group claims to have recorded the sounds of cannonballs and musket fire and has photographed misty figures said to be ghosts.

The Manassas Battlefield, in Prince William County, is also home to a number of Civil War spirits. During the Second Battle of Manassas, in 1862, the Fifth New York Volunteer Infantry (Zouaves) sustained devastating losses. One veteran wrote, "Where the Regiment stood that day was the very vortex of Hell. Not only were men wounded, or killed, but they were

A phantom New York Zouave soldier has been seen repeatedly on the Manassas Battlefield.

riddled." One of the dead may still haunt the area. A phantom Zouave soldier has been seen repeatedly on the battlefield's New York Avenue Field. The phantom beckons the onlooker to follow him into the woods. To date, no one has taken the ghost up on the offer.

Near the New York Avenue Field, a structure known as the Old Stone House is also said to be haunted. Originally a tavern, the house served as a field hospital during both the Battles of First (1861) and Second (1862) Manassas. Strange lights have been seen in the house at night, although it is locked every night by park rangers. Strange sounds, like screams and groans, are also said to come from the house.

The Cold Harbor Battlefield in Hanover County is said to top the list of haunted battlefields in Virginia. Here in 1864, thousands of Union troops were killed as wave after wave of men were repeatedly thrown in frontal assaults against fortified Confederate positions. Today, some visitors claim to have felt the thunder of artillery and smelled burned gunpowder while exploring the battlefield. Once again, the shouts and cries of unseen combatants echo through the woods. Visitors report the sudden appearance

Buildings used as field hospitals, such as the Old Stone House in Manassas, are often said to be haunted.

of a dense fog on the battlefield, which just as quickly disappears. The ghostly fog has driven away many who seek the safety of their cars, even as they hear unearthly footsteps behind them and sense unseen eyes on them.

Hauntings are also reported in buildings used during the Civil War as hospitals. One house in Brandy Station, Culpeper County, was used as a hospital after the Battle of Brandy Station (June 9, 1863). The patients scrawled their names and other thoughts on the walls; thus, the house is now known as the Graffiti House. So troubling were the ongoing ghostly occurrences at the Graffiti House that the Virginia Paranormal Institute was called in to conduct an investigation. One investigator felt an unseen force tightening around her wrist. Another person saw a picture frame move on its own. The team's electrical instruments raced out of control.

Another Civil War hospital of long standing was set up in Gordonsville, Orange County. Gordonsville's Exchange Hotel opened in 1860 and provided an elegant stopping place for passengers on the Virginia Central Railway. In March 1862, the Confederate army transformed the hotel into the Gordonsville Receiving Hospital. Dr. B.M. Lebby of South Carolina was the director of the hospital, and its operations continued under his leadership until October 1865.

The wounded and dying from nearby battlefields such as Cedar Mountain, Chancellorsville, Brandy Station and the Wilderness were brought to Gordonsville by the trainloads. Although this was primarily a Confederate facility, the hospital treated the wounded from both sides. By the end of the war, more than seventy thousand men had been treated at the Gordonsville Receiving Hospital, and over seven hundred were buried on its surrounding grounds and later interred at Maplewood Cemetery in Gordonsville.

The Exchange Hotel Civil War Medical Museum, as the structure is known today, has experienced more than one ghostly occurrence. Screams and groans are heard, doors close on their own and eerie orbs appear suddenly in rooms. Some have claimed they have encountered nurses, garbed in black, wandering the halls.

There are reports of ghostly happenings at Civil War sites all over Virginia. How do we account for such stories? The two most often reported types of hauntings are categorized as residual hauntings and intelligent hauntings. Residual hauntings are the most common form of hauntings and may eventually be found to be natural phenomena. A residual haunting is similar to a DVD that is played over and over again. In a residual American Civil War battlefield haunting, for example, the sights, sounds and even smells of battle are continually replayed and are always the same. Apparitions may be seen, but they will not notice living people around them. The theory here is that energy created by the strong emotions created in battle imprints itself on a physical place and that an individual sensitive enough to pick up this embedded energy sees and hears ghostly events, while those who lack such sensitivity do not. Since current science has no instruments to measure such embedded energy or test for individual psychic sensitivity to that energy, such hauntings are dismissed out of hand, even though they may actually exist.

Intelligent hauntings, which are reported much less frequently than residual hauntings, involve a ghost being aware of the living world and interacting with it. Interactions may involve speaking and moving inanimate objects around the room.

Of course, reports of ghostly activity are not confined to Civil War battlefields and hospitals. Throw a stone in Virginia and you are apt to hit a ghost. In his book *Haunted Prince William County* (The History Press, 2020), author Andrew Mills notes ghosts in the following towns and villages of Prince William County: Dumfries has three ghosts, Occoquan has two ghosts, Haymarket has six ghosts, Bristow has two ghosts, Manassas has three ghosts (not including the battlefield ghosts) and Nokesville has one ghost. There are literally hundreds of ghosts roaming about Virginia. The following are accounts of some of the most famous ones.

Avenel Plantation, in Bedford County, hosts some interesting and talkative ghosts. Paranormal investigators have come away with a number of recordings of ghostly chatter, some of which are intelligible. One ghost purportedly said, "The secret is in the wall," which is intriguing, while another ghost said, "Here kitty, kitty, kitty," which is not nearly as intriguing. Paranormal investigators took pictures of a floating orb that supposedly looked like an eye. Of course, all of the investigators heard strange noises, and some became dizzy. Lights suddenly go on in the house, and visitors have reported smells, like the strong smell of tobacco and whiffs of perfume, even though no other living person is present. Letitia Burwell is the house's most famous ghostly resident. Known as the "Lady in White," the ghost of Letitia Burwell glides through the halls and around the grounds of the estate. She is often seen carrying a parasol.

Shirley Plantation in Charles City County boasts the presence of a haunted painting. The painting is the portrait of a woman, an ancient aunt, which hung in a place of honor for many years until it was stored in the attic in 1858. It was then that strange knocking sounds started coming from the attic. The noise grew louder every day until the painting was restored to its rightful place, at which point the knocking stopped. Over one hundred years later, the painting was shipped to New York City to be displayed as a paranormal curiosity at a conference. The painting began shaking violently while on display. Once the painting was returned to its accustomed place in Virginia, all paranormal activity ceased.

The Abijah Thomas House, known as the Octagon House, in Adwolf, Smyth County, has a sinister history. Built in 1857, the seventeen-room house has within it a place called "the dark room," a former storage room where Abijah Thomas tortured slaves. The ghosts of these slaves haunt the old house, dripping blood, still wearing the heavy chains of their enslavement.

Tuckahoe Plantation in Henrico County is home to the ghost of a brokenhearted woman. Forced to marry against her will, the poor woman led a life of misery and despair with a cruel and despotic husband. Her spirit wanders through the plantation grounds, still the captive of her earthly prison.

Perhaps the most haunted house in Virginia is Ferry Plantation House in Virginia Beach, which boasts no fewer than eleven ghostly residents. Among those haunting the house are a slave named Henry, a woman who died after falling down the stairs, a painter named Thomas Williamson, a brokenhearted lover named Sally and victims of a shipwreck that occurred nearby. People have seen ghostly apparitions and heard strange noises. Lights go on by themselves. Balls of light have been seen dancing on the roof.

Virginia ghosts—real or imagined? Investigate more deeply, if you dare.

EDGAR CAYCE, THE "SLEEPING PROPHET"

Edgar Cayce, who by the 1940s was known as the "Miracle Man of Virginia Beach," began to demonstrate remarkable psychic abilities at an early age in Kentucky. A poor student, the young Cayce had a talent that any student would admire: he could fall asleep on a book and wake up with a photographic memory of every word in the book. His sleeping powers soon extended beyond memorizing books. As a boy, he became very ill after being struck by a baseball. He diagnosed his own problem in his sleep. When a member of the family became ill, his father asked young Edgar to diagnose the problem. Edgar went to sleep and not only diagnosed the problem but also prescribed the cure. After this, the local doctor began to rely on his advice.

Edgar took up photography as a business, married and moved away. When his wife, suffering from tuberculosis, was given up for dead by the doctors, Edgar went to sleep and received specific directions on how to cure her. She eventually made a complete recovery, and Edgar Cayce committed to understanding and using his powers. The remedies Cayce channeled often involved alternative forms of medicine such as energy medicine. Cayce's readings often spoke of the role played by vibrations. According to Cayce, there is a type of consciousness in each individual atom, and just as a musical instrument can get out of tune, so, too, can the human body. Healing depends on reestablishing harmonious vibrations.

As Cayce's fame spread, newspapers began running stories about the "illiterate man [who] becomes a doctor when hypnotized." Cayce was described as a "psychic diagnostician" and the "Sleeping Prophet." This is how he worked. A person would come to consult Cayce. Cayce would recline on a couch and promptly fall asleep. Moments later, his eyes would open and he would start reciting diagnoses and cures, notwithstanding the fact that he had absolutely no medical training. Even more amazing was the fact that the person for whom Cayce was reading did not have to be present. All Cayce needed for a successful reading was the person's name and current location. The theory behind this "distance healing" is that the healer projects thoughts toward both the sick person and the spiritual world. The healer establishes a link between the two, and the healing energies of the universe begin to flow. The healer acts as a bridge between spirit and flesh.

In 1925, Cayce received spiritual guidance to move to Virginia Beach, where he would live for the next twenty years. By this time, Edgar was a well-respected psychic with numerous followers (some wealthy) and a small number of full-time employees and volunteers working with him. It was in Virginia Beach that Edgar Cayce began the institutions that survived him, most notably the Association for Research and Enlightenment, which preserves, in minute detail, the proceedings of over fourteen thousand readings done by Cayce.

During the years of World War II, Edgar Cayce did some 1,385 readings. He collapsed under the strain and died on January 3, 1945.

While Edgar Cayce left an amazing record of correct medical diagnoses, he also ventured into other areas. Readings also dealt with reincarnation, the nature of synchronicity, soul mates and other exotic subjects such as the existence of the advanced civilization of Atlantis twelve thousand years ago. He also made predictions about future events. Supposedly, he predicted World War II years before it happened. His 1935 prediction reads:

The activities that have already begun have assumed such proportions that there is to be the attempt upon the part of groups to penalize, or to make for the associations of groups to carry on same. This will make for the taking of sides, as it were, by various groups or countries or governments. This will be indicated by the Austrians, Germans, and later the Japanese joining in their influence; unseen, and gradually growing to those affairs where there must become, as it were, almost a direct opposition to that which has been the THEME of the Nazis (the Aryan). For these will gradually make for a growing of animosities.

And unless there is interference from what may be called by many the supernatural forces and influences, that are active in the affairs of nations and peoples, the whole world—as it were—will be set on fire by the militaristic groups and those that are "for" power and expansion in such associations.

While World War II did occur, you didn't need to have psychic powers in 1935 to know that there was trouble on the horizon as dictators started flexing their muscles. Other predictions were just flat out wrong, like the discovery of Atlantis before the year 2000.

Edgar Cayce also conducted a psychic reading on February 1, 1944, concerning Arizona's legendary "Lost Dutchman's Mine." Cayce said:

In undertaking directions for location of this from the present conditions, many things should be taken into consideration—as to whether descriptions would apply to those periods when this was put in the way of being hidden and/or those that would apply to the present day surroundings. For time in its essence—while it is one, in space there has been made a great variation by the activities of the elements and the characters that have been in these areas. For these are held as sacred grounds by groups who have, from period to period, changed the very face of the earth or the surroundings, for the very purpose of being misleading to those who might attempt to discover or to desecrate (to certain groups) those lands.

As we find, if we would locate this—from the present outlook: We would go from the cactus marked here, in Canyon, some 5, 10, 20, 30, 37½ yards to the north by west—north by west—to a place where, on the side of the hills, there is a white rock—almost pure white—almost as a triangle on top. Turn from here—for you can't get over some of the ground going directly to the east—turn almost directly to the east, and just where there is crossing of the deep gulch, we will find the entrance to the Dutch Mine. This has been covered over, though to begin at the lower portion of the gulch we would find only about six feet before we would reach pay dirt in gold.

Whether it was common sense or psychic ability, Cayce's reading hit on two rather obvious points. The terrain around the Lost Dutchman's Mine has changed since the 1890s. Earthquakes may have significantly disturbed any clues left behind. Additionally, the many treasure hunters who have walked the ground may have altered or removed clues to mislead competitors. It isn't clear if anyone has followed up on the directions provided by Edgar Cayce, but if they have, they are playing it pretty close to the vest.

STRANGE TALES

PRESIDENTIAL LORE

Virginia is often called the "Mother of Presidents," having produced more presidents than any other state in the Union. Each of these presidents has left behind some interesting personal lore. Take, for example, George Washington, the first president. Born in Westmoreland County, Washington became the iconic "Indispensable Man." Artists and poets went to outlandish lengths to deify the man. In 1832, Horatio Greenough was commissioned by Congress to produce a marble statue of Washington. It turned out to be quite a statue. Greenough produced a statue based on the great statue of Zeus, one of the Seven Wonders of the Ancient World. Washington is seated, bare chested, in Roman clothing and pointing toward heaven. Initially meant for the Capitol Rotunda, the statue soon created an uproar. Many found the half-dressed Washington offensive; others found him comical. Some wags suggested that Washington was reaching for his clothes. The statue was booted out of the Rotunda and placed on the grounds of the Capitol, where it continued to raise controversy. The statue was next housed at the Patent Office before finding a permanent home at the Smithsonian Institution.

Here are some other fun facts. Most people think Washington wore a white wig, but he didn't. Washington had his own hair powdered frequently, which was the custom of the time. The powder made his real hair look white. Washington is said to have thrown a silver dollar across the Potomac, but he didn't. He actually hurled a stone across the much narrower Rappahannock River in Fredericksburg.

America's third president, Thomas Jefferson, author of the Declaration of Independence, was born in Albemarle County. Here are the ten precepts that the philosophical "Sage of Monticello" left behind to guide us through life:

(1) Never put off till tomorrow what you can do today. (2) Never trouble another for what you can do yourself. (3) Never spend your money before you have it. (4) Never buy what you do not want, because it is cheap: it will be dear to you. (5) Pride costs us more than hunger, thirst, or cold. (6) We never repent of having eaten too little. (7) Nothing is troublesome that we do willingly. (8) How much pain has cost us the evils which have never happened! (9) Take things always by their smooth handle. (10) When angry count to ten before you speak; if very angry, to a hundred.

Jefferson loathed pomp and circumstance and was having none of it when it came time for his inauguration. Jefferson is said to have ridden to the Capitol, hitched his horse to a fence and walked in unattended to take the oath of office. Jefferson wanted no respect shown to him that he would not be entitled to as an ordinary citizen. Jefferson died on July 4, 1826, the fiftieth anniversary of the Declaration of Independence.

James Madison created the basic framework for the U.S. Constitution and was America's fourth president. Born in King George County, James Madison was the shortest president, standing five feet, four inches tall and weighing in at about one hundred pounds. Madison was a sickly individual given to sudden seizures and attacks of "bilious fever." Madison's voice was so weak that people had difficulty hearing what he said. Despite his physical frailty, Madison served two full terms and outlived two vice presidents. Madison's first vice president died in 1812. The next vice president died eighteen months later. Madison completed his second term without a vice president. He died in 1836 at the age of eighty-five.

During the War of 1812, the sickly James Madison became the only sitting U.S. president to directly participate in a military action. The British landed at Benedict, Maryland, on August 19, 1814, achieving complete tactical surprise. The British marched rapidly north. Madison borrowed a pair of dueling pistols and set out to rally the American militia. The president was so far forward that he almost blundered into the British army. When battle was joined on August 24, the outcome was a foregone conclusion. Some 4,500 British veterans faced 429 American regulars and 1,500 poorly trained and poorly equipped militia in a set piece battle in the open. After losing 10 dead

James Madison was the shortest president, standing five feet, four inches tall and weighing in at about one hundred pounds.

and 40 wounded, the Americans fled the field, leaving ten cannons behind. The rout was complete and was derided at the time as the "Bladensburg Races." The remnants of the American army fled toward Washington, with the British in hot pursuit.

The British burned the city of Washington. The glow from the burning city could be seen forty miles away in Baltimore. With the city of Washington in flames, President Madison and twenty-two wagonloads of United States documents—including the Declaration of Independence, the Articles of Confederation, the Constitution, much of George Washington's correspondences and Congressional and State Department records—made their way across the Potomac River into Virginia. Loudoun County served briefly as a temporary refuge for both President Madison and the important state papers. The Constitution and other state papers were brought to a plantation called Rokeby, near Leesburg, where they were stored in a vaulted room in the cellar. President Madison established headquarters at Belmont, where he was the guest of Ludwell Lee. Local tradition holds that, since all of the government's documents were stored at Rokeby House, Leesburg was briefly the capital of the United States.

James Monroe, born in Westmoreland County, was America's fifth president and father of the Monroe Doctrine, one of the pillars of American foreign policy designed to prevent the interference of foreign powers in the affairs of the Western Hemisphere. Monroe was very popular in his day. He was elected to his first term in 1816 in a landslide victory in which he received 68 percent of the vote. In 1820, he ran unopposed, the only president other than George Washington to have ever done so. One elector from New Hampshire kept Monroe from winning a unanimous vote in the Electoral College. Three Founding Fathers who became president died on July 4. Thomas Jefferson and John Adams both died on July 4, 1826. Monroe died on July 4, 1831.

William Henry Harrison, born in Charles City County, was America's ninth president. Harrison was also the shortest serving president, dying thirty-one days into his first term. A military hero in his younger days, the new president wanted to demonstrate his virility when he came to Washington. He took the oath of office outside on a cold, wet day without wearing a hat or overcoat. Harrison's inaugural speech dragged on for almost two hours (the longest inaugural speech ever given), after which Harrison rode a horse in his own inaugural parade. On March 26, Harrison was ill with cold-like symptoms. The next day, he developed chills and then a high fever. The doctors were called in to treat the ailing president. As

WILLIAM HENRY HARRISON.
Ninth President of the United States.

Pub. by N. Currier. 2 Spruce St N.Y.

The death of William Henry Harrison in office gave rise to the legend of a curse on the presidency.

was often the case in those days, calling in the doctors was tantamount to signing the man's death warrant. A team of doctors administered a regimen of bloodletting to drain off the "bad humors." When this failed to produce the desired results, the doctors tried ipecac, castor oil, calomel, mustard plasters, a boiled mixture of crude petroleum and Virginia snakeroot. All of this expert medical treatment only weakened Harrison to the point of death, at which point the doctors concluded that he was beyond hope and would not recover.

William Henry Harrison was the first president to die in office, and around his death arose the legend of the Curse of Tippecanoe. Harrison had become famous as a military commander in Tecumseh's War, waged against the great Shawnee leader Tecumseh and his brother Tenskwatawa. The decisive battle of that war was the Battle of Tippecanoe, and it was the fame Harrison won in this battle that helped propel "Old Tippecanoe" into the White House under the campaign slogan "Tippecanoe and Tyler too." In what became known as Tecumseh's Curse, a grim pattern emerged after the election of 1840: death stalked any person elected president in a year divisible by twenty. William Henry Harrison: elected in 1840, died in office. Abraham Lincoln: elected in 1860, died in office. James A. Garfield: elected in 1880, died in office. William McKinley: elected in 1900, died in office. Warren G. Harding: elected in 1920, died in office. Franklin D. Roosevelt: elected in 1940, died in office. John F. Kennedy: elected in 1960, died in office. Ronald Reagan: elected in 1980—broke the curse. Reagan served two terms and lived fifteen years after leaving the presidency.

John Tyler, born in Charles City County, was William Henry Harrison's vice president and the first vice president to succeed to the presidency because of the death of the president. Tyler's actions after the death of Harrison set an important precedent for the future. Tyler immediately took the oath of office, moved into the White House and began to act as though he had been elected. These actions had no foundation in law, but the precedent that Tyler established endured for 150 years before the rules for the presidential succession were established in law by the Twenty-Fifth Amendment to the Constitution, ratified in 1967.

John Tyler was not a popular president. Most of his cabinet quickly resigned because of his highhanded methods. Dubbed "His Accidency," Tyler was expelled from his own party and was unable to find any existing party willing to nominate him when he tried to run for a full term of his own in 1844. When the American Civil War broke out, Tyler ran for and was elected to the House of Representatives of the Confederate States of

America. John Tyler died in 1862 and is generally not considered one of the better presidents.

Zachary Taylor, the nation's twelfth president, was born in Orange County. Taylor was a career military officer and played an important role in the Mexican-American War. As president, he is chiefly remembered for dying after eating a huge bowl of cherries on a hot summer day.

Woodrow Wilson, the nation's twenty-eighth president, was born in Staunton and led the country during World War I. Stress related to Wilson's tireless efforts trying to win support for a postwar League of Nations caused him to have a series of strokes. The now frail and partially incapacitated Wilson refused to resign and remained in office until the end of his second term in 1921. There were no provisions in law at that time for removing an incapacitated president from office (the rules for the presidential succession were established in law by the Twenty-Fifth Amendment to the Constitution, ratified in 1967), so there arose the legend that the first lady, Edith Bolling Galt Wilson, became the de facto president of the United States. According to this story, Edith Wilson controlled access to the ailing president and shaped the major decisions of his last years in office. "The Secret President" or "First Woman President," as she has been called, was from Virginia, born in Wytheville in 1872. In her 1939 memoirs, Mrs. Wilson states that her husband's doctors urged her "stewardship" on her.

Another fun fact about Woodrow and Edith Wilson: when Woodrow Wilson returned from the Paris Peace Conference of 1919, he was greeted by cheering crowds and a gleaming new Pierce-Arrow limousine. Leased by the U.S. government, this car quickly became President Wilson's favorite. One of the finest luxury cars of the day, Pierce-Arrow sold cars to the emperor of Japan, the shah of Persia, the king of Greece and royalty throughout Europe and the Middle East. The company was often referred to as the "American Rolls-Royce." When Wilson left office, five of his wealthy Princeton classmates bought the car and presented it as a gift to the ex-president. Although he was the first president to join the American Automobile Association (AAA), Wilson never had a driver's license. His wife, Edith, however, owned and drove her own electric car.

THE REMEUM

An urban legend spread throughout local high schools in Virginia during the 1950s to 1970s of a place called "The Crypts" where teenagers could go in the dead of night for sex, drugs, booze and vandalism. A host of lesser urban legends sprang from the Crypts, including:

The caretaker lived in a house next to the crypts and was called Stumpy because he had no legs below his knees, just a board nailed between his stumps. He got around in a wheel chair pulled by mad dogs who he would sic on kids who walked down the gravel road to the crypts at night. He also had a shot gun loaded with rock salt.

The statue of Admiral Remey had its head stolen by some kid from a neighboring school. The kid was then killed by being decapitated in a car accident.

The crypts were vast with several levels. Almost everyone knew "some guy" who had been down to the lower levels using a secret door in the floor. No one could find the door.

Hell's Angels (or the Pagans) blew up the crypts with dynamite after the cops bothered them too many times while partying there.

The Remeum was a family mausoleum built to rival the tombs of the Egyptian pharaohs. *Author's collection.*

Although no one can vouch for the authenticity of these tales, the Crypts themselves were, in fact, real and located in Lorton, Virginia. "The Crypts" refers to a place known to history as the Remeum. The Remeum was a huge family mausoleum erected on land belonging to Pohick Church by controversial Baha'i faith leader Charles Mason Remey.

Charles Mason Remey was born in Burlington, Iowa, on May 15, 1874. Remey's father was a highly decorated U.S. Naval officer from a wealthy family. His mother also came from a wealthy family. The young Remey trained as an architect at Cornell University (1893–96) before leaving to attend the prestigious Ecole des Beaux-Arts in Paris, France (1896–1903). He studied widely and became an assistant professor of architecture at George Washington University from 1904 to 1908 and then toured the world studying Oriental architecture. While studying in Paris, Remey became interested in the Baha'i World Faith, in which he subsequently became a leading figure. He was chosen to design Baha'i temples in Israel, Iran and Australia.

In 1932, Remey married Gertrude Heim Klemm Mason, and the couple settled into a palatial home on Massachusetts Avenue in Washington, D.C.

There they entertained Washington's elite. Within a year of their marriage, Gertrude died under mysterious circumstances. The official version listed her death as a suicide, but some have questioned how she could have shot herself in the head twice at point blank range with a large .45-caliber pistol.

During World War II, Remey dealt directly with British spymaster Sir William Stephenson, FBI director J. Edgar Hoover and the head of American wartime intelligence, William "Wild Bill" Donovan, in getting Baha'i faithful out of Nazi-occupied Europe. In the late 1940s, Remey used his connection to Alan Dulles, head of the Central Intelligence Agency, to help secure the Baha'i property and holy sites when the state of Israel was being created.

In 1960, Charles Mason Remey declared himself head of the Baha'i faith, causing a major schism within the faith and embroiling Remey in controversy for the rest of his life. Remey was an individual with a large ego. If his unilateral assumption of the title "Hereditary Guardian" of the Baha'i faith did not demonstrate this, then his second great passion, the building of a family mausoleum (the Remeum) to rival the tombs of the Egyptian pharaohs, did.

The Remeum was constructed over a twenty-year period (1937–58) until a disagreement between the Pohick Church and Remey resulted in legal action. The mausoleum was designed by Charles Remey as a memorial to his family's contributions to America. Remey transported the bodies of fifteen relatives and enshrined them in the Remeum.

According to the Washington *Evening Star and Daily News* of April 9, 1973, the mausoleum was planned as a "magnificent complex of walled courtyards, underground chambers with soaring vaulted ceilings, marble reliefs and statues, carved pillars, chapels and burial vaults." Remey devoted most of his large fortune to building this burial complex. Some two million bricks were used in its construction. Remey planned to build a huge three-story structure above the underground mausoleum, which would have dwarfed Pohick Church.

The completed sections of the Remeum complex included outer courtyards, an atrium and the underground mausoleum. Costing millions of dollars, the complex featured bas reliefs and sculptures by the famous American sculptor Felix de Weldon, who created the iconic flag-raising Iwo Jima U.S. Marine Corps memorial located in Rosslyn, Virginia. There were also sculptures by other artists decorating the various tombs, alcoves and hallways of the gargantuan structure. Historic events in which the Remey family participated, from the landing of the Pilgrims to Pearl Harbor, were depicted. Two massive sleeping lions sculpted by Felix de Weldon guarded the entrance to the mausoleum. Inside the memorial chapel were life-size statues depicting "Faith" and "Charity." Another series of carved reliefs illustrated the lives of saints. The complex was lit by electric chandeliers and had an extensive ventilation system and plumbing.

Charles Mason Remey wrote of his creation, "In these later days the further that one can burrow down into the ground the safer is one's construction from atomic danger as well as natural disintegration....I am trusting if such a catastrophe should strike Washington [an atomic blast] that the chambers of the Remeum that are below ground would survive."

Built to survive an atomic war, the Remeum did not survive teenage vandals and motorcycle gangs. Unguarded in what was then rural Virginia, the Remeum was frequently vandalized. Hundreds of vandals defaced the complex over the years. Fragments of smashed marble reliefs and statues littered the floors. Discarded beer cans and whiskey bottles were mixed with broken funeral urns and the ashes of the dead. Statues too large to steal were chipped or painted. With construction halted, Remey relinquished all rights to the Pohick Church in 1968. Remey was given five years to remove anything of value from the mausoleum. Remey's brother-in-law, a navy admiral, transferred the remains of fifteen family members to Pompey, New York. Remey's wife, Gertrude, was reinterred in the Pohick Church Cemetery. The marker over her grave appears to be a marble plaque from the Remeum. The complex was dismantled over a period of ten years, being finally bulldozed over in 1983. Currently, the only remaining features of the Remeum are an obelisk honoring Remey's father and mother that stood at one end of the courtyard, south of the inner atrium's entrance, and two chimney/vent structures. The area has been reforested since the 1983 bulldozing, and there are no other visible traces of the complex left.

STUDYING REINCARNATION
IN VIRGINIA

The French philosopher Voltaire observed that it would be no more surprising to be born twice than to be born once. Buddhists and Hindus believe in reincarnation. Some European Christians believed in reincarnation until the church banned such beliefs in AD 553. Despite the widespread interest and belief in reincarnation, there had been no scientific investigation of reincarnation until the task was taken up by Dr. Ian Stevenson of the University of Virginia.

In 1957, Dr. Stevenson (1918–2007) was named head of the Department of Psychiatry at the University of Virginia, where he began to seriously investigate the subject of reincarnation. In 1968, Chester Carlson, the inventor of the Xerox copying process, bequeathed $1 million (equivalent to $75 million in today's money) to the university on condition that the money be used to fund Stevenson's work. The new research group was called the Division of Personality Studies (renamed the Division of Perceptual Studies in 2004) and is the only university-based research unit in the world devoted to the study of previous life memories and near-death experiences.

By collecting thousands of cases of children who spontaneously, without hypnosis, remembered a past life, Dr. Stevenson offered convincing scientific evidence, if not proof, of reincarnation. In each case of a child's past life memory, Dr. Stevenson methodically documented the child's statements. He then identified the deceased person the child remembered being and verified the facts of the deceased person's life that matched the child's memory. He even matched birthmarks and birth defects to wounds and scars on the

The Division of Perceptual Studies is the only university-based research unit devoted to the study of reincarnation.

deceased, verified by medical records. His strict methods systematically ruled out all possible "normal" explanations for the child's memories. Dr. Stevenson devoted forty years to the scientific documentation of past life memories of children from all over the world, documenting some three thousand cases in his files. Many people, including skeptics and scholars, agree that these cases offer the best evidence yet for reincarnation.

Stevenson found cases on five continents. Most were found in cultures in which the idea of reincarnation is widely accepted, places like India and Lebanon. The cases Stevenson investigated most intensely were those in which it could be reliably established that the life a child claimed to recall belonged to a stranger, unknown to the child's family or anyone the family had contact with. These were cases, according to a *Washington Post* article dated August 8, 1999, like that of the girl who kept telephoning "Leila." In this case, a middle-class girl living in Beirut, Lebanon, believed that she remembered the life of a woman who had died undergoing heart surgery in Richmond, Virginia. At the age of sixteen months, the girl pulled the phone off the hook and said, "Hello, Leila?" over and over. The girl claimed she was

Leila's mother. The behavior continued, and the girl mentioned the names of thirteen close relatives of the dead woman. She finally begged her parents to take her to her "real" home. When the family arrived in Richmond, they found that the details given by the girl were accurate. They also learned that minutes before undergoing her heart surgery, the dead woman had tried to call her daughter Leila.

Dr. Stevenson published only for the academic and scientific community. He shunned the mainstream media, afraid that it would sensationalize his research. His writing is dry, technical and difficult for the average reader. His scientific approach to the subject made him skeptical of accounts of previous lives obtained by hypnosis or "past life regression." He kept a file in his office that he labeled "Extravagant Claims."

In 1997, Dr. Stevenson published a 2,268-page, two-volume work called *Reincarnation and Biology*. In this work, Stevenson identified a number of patterns among the cases. Typically, children only between the ages of two and seven spoke of past lives. Stevenson also found that strong emotions, such as traumatic death, related to a child's remembering a past life. He also reported that reincarnation was not immediate; there was usually a gap of several years between lives.

Dr. Stevenson saw his job as that of gathering data regarding past life memories, investigating the data and ruling out every possible rational explanation. His greatest frustration was that many scientists dismissed his work without even bothering to read the evidence. Stevenson once said, "The wish not to believe can influence as strongly as the wish to believe." Doris Kuhlmann-Wilsdorf was one scientist who did examine the evidence and wrote that Stevenson's work establishes that "the statistical probability that reincarnation does in fact occur is so overwhelming…that cumulatively the evidence is not inferior to that for most if not all branches of science."

The jury still appears to be out. Dr. Harold Lief wrote in the *Journal of Nervous and Mental Disease*, "Either Dr. Stevenson is making a colossal mistake, or he will be known as the Galileo of the 20th century."

TOO GOOD TO BE TRUE

In 1885, Zebulon Miller of Lynchburg died. Before he died, Miller built a concrete mausoleum with three-foot-thick walls. He directed in his will that $2.3 million in gold and silver coins be installed along with his body in the mausoleum. A trust was set up that paid for armed guards, who were later replaced by a high-tech security system. Miller and his fortune rest happily together for all eternity. So goes the legend. But this legend can be traced back to a fairly recent source, the website of "'Little-Known' Attractions of Lynchburg and Central Virginia" (www.retroweb. com/lynchburg/attractions/main.html).

Real-life journalist Darell Laurant, of the actual Lynchburg newspaper the *News & Advance*, writes that the website "has a genius for coming up with people, landmarks and historical events that are just too weird to be real. And with good reason." Relying on Photoshop and good writing that just touches the unbelievable but never quite goes over the line, the website creates an alternate reality where we can't be sure what is true and what is totally made up.

Other stories include such gems as "Evington's Lost Locomotive." On February 5, 1952, a Ringling Brothers and Barnum & Bailey's Circus train derailed in Evington, just outside Lynchburg. Thirty-five gorillas escaped, and none were ever recovered. The gorillas lived in the woods in and around Campbell County for the next thirty years, where they harassed the locals and family pets and stole from gardens. The last report of gorilla-related activity was in 1981. One picture exists from 1967, when Horace Dalrymple found one of the gorillas on his roof. Of course, if you dig further, you will find that there was no train derailment in Virginia in 1952 and that the story is a concoction of our friend at "'Little-Known' Attractions of Lynchburg and Central Virginia."

Tales such as these seem to be confusing people on the internet. One story in particular, the story of the "Elon Obelisk," has created much wonder, probably because people want so much to believe. According to this story, there stands in a dense wooded area near Elon one of central Virginia's greatest mysteries: a seventy-five-foot-tall stone obelisk resembling something Mayan from the jungles of Central America. The ancient pillar, deteriorating over the

A circus train derailed just outside Lynchburg. Thirty-five gorillas escaped, and none were ever recovered.

centuries, first came to public attention in a photo that appeared in a 1964 issue of *National Geographic*. In 1972, the Elon Obelisk Society was founded to study the mystery. One inquisitive soul sent out a request on the internet that reads, "Need help locating a piece of local legend. I've lived in a town called Elon all my life....A few years ago I read about an obelisk that was discovered in my town, in the mountains, of unknown origin. It's simply called the 'Elon Obelisk' and there's even an 'Elon Obelisk Society' around."

Expect to see the legends of Zebulon Miller's Tomb, Evington's Lost Locomotive and the Elon Obelisk passed down as stories based on historical "facts" one hundred years from now.

SELECTED BIBLIOGRAPHY

Books

Brady, Patricia. *Martha Washington: An American Life*. New York: Penguin, 2006.

Bryan, Helen. *Martha Washington: First Lady of Liberty*. New York: John Wiley, 2002.

Cayton, M.K., E.J. Goran and P.W. Williams, eds. *Encyclopedia of American Social History*. Vol. III. New York: Scribners, 1993.

Davis, Burke. *The Long Surrender*. New York: Random House, 1985.

Hart, George L. *The Beale Papers*. N.p.: privately published, 1964.

Innis, P.B., and Walter Dean Innis. *Gold in the Blue Ridge*. Washington, D.C.: Devon Publishing Co., 1973.

Jensen, Amy La Folette. *The White House and Its Thirty-Three Families*. New York: McGraw Hill, 1962.

Jones, John B. *A Rebel War Clerk's Diary*. New York: A.S. Barnes, 1961.

Marinucci, Kathy W., ed. *Fairfax County Stories 1607–2007*. Fairfax, VA: Fairfax County Board of Supervisors, 2007.

Marx, Robert F. *Buried Treasures of the United States*. New York: David McKay Company, 1978.

Meany, Marion, and Mary Lipsey. *Braddock's True Gold*. Fairfax, VA: Fairfax County Board of Supervisors, 2006.

Perkin, Joan. *Victorian Women*. New York: New York University Press, 1995.

Schama, Simon. *Rough Crossing*. New York: HarperCollins, 2007.

Traylor, Waverly. *The Great Dismal Swamp in Myth and Legend*. Pittsburgh, PA: Rose Dog Press, 2010.

Wiencek, Henry. *An Imperfect God: George Washington, His Slaves, and the Creation of America*. New York: Straus and Giroux, 2003.

Williams, Lloyd Haynes. *Pirates of Colonial Virginia*. Richmond, VA: Dietz Press, 1937.

Articles

Biddle, Francis. "Scandal at Bizarre." *American Heritage* 12, no. 5 (1961).

Daniloff, R. "Cipher's the Key to the Treasure in Them Thar Hills." *Smithsonian Magazine*, April 1981.

Doyle, Christopher L. "The Randolph Scandal in Early National Virginia, 1792–1815." *Journal of Southern History*, May 1, 2003.

Lemay, J.A. Leo. "Robert Bolling and the Bailment of Colonel Chiswell." *Early American Literature* 6 (1971).

Websites

Andrews, Evan. "10 Things You May Not Know About James Madison." History.com.www.history.com/news/10-things-you-may-not-know-about-jamesmadison#:~:text=8.,involved%20in%20a%20military%20engagement.

Bass, Nikki. "The Firebird Legend." Descendants of the Great Dismal. descendantsofthegreatdismal.com/2020/03/23/the-firebird-legend.

Berry, Jesse. "Ian Stevenson's Case for the Afterlife." Scientific American, November 2, 2013. blogs.scientificamerican.com/bering-in-mind/ian-stevensone28099s-case-for-the-afterlife-are-we-e28098skepticse28099-really-just-cynics.

Black Loyalist Heritage Society. www.blackloyalist.com.

Boyd, Bentley. "Mystery Vault May Yield Papers of Francis Bacon." *Baltimore Sun*, August 21, 1992. www.baltimoresun.com/news/bs-xpm-1992-08-21-1992234043-story.html.

Cayce.com. cayce.com/news/miracle-man-virginia-beach.

Chincoteague.com. www.chincoteague.com/ponies.html.

Civil War Women. civilwarwomenblog.com/civil-war-women-doctors.

Colonial Ghosts. colonialghosts.com/top-25-most-haunted-places-in-virginia.

EdgarCayce.org. www.edgarcayce.org/the-readings/health-and-wellness/ holistic-health-database/health-and-healing-introduction.

Fairfax Underground. "The Remey Tomb/Crypt." www.fairfaxunderground. com/forum/read/2/281023/page-1.html.

Geiling, Natasha. "The (Still) Mysterious Death of Edgar Allan Poe." *Smithsonian Magazine*, October 7, 2014. www.smithsonianmag.com/ history/still-mysterious-death-edgar-allan-poe-180952936.

Harki, Gary. "Spooky Tales from the Great Dismal Swamp." *Virginia Pilot*, October 14, 2014. www.pilotonline.com/life/article_71c5f7f3-5e8f-5370-918b-00ecf1101102.html.

Legends of America. www.legendsofamerica.com/na-powhatan.

"'Little-Known' Attractions of Lynchburg and Central Virginia." www. retroweb.com/lynchburg/attractions/main.html.

Monticello. www.monticello.org.

Montpelier. www.montpelier.org.

Morgan, Thad. "How a Black Spy Infiltrated the Confederate White House." History.com, January 21, 2020. www.history.com/news/female-spies-civil-war-mary-bowser-elizabeth-van-lew.

Mount Vernon. www.mountvernon.org.

National Constitution Center. "10 Birthday Facts about President James Monroe." April 28, 2020. constitutioncenter.org/blog/10-surprising-birthday-facts-about-james-monroe.

PBS Frontline. "George & Venus." PBS. www.pbs.org.

Pompeian, Ed. "George Washington's Slave Child?" History News Network, George Mason University, March 21, 2005. hnn.us.

Powhatan Museum. www.powhatanmuseum.com/Michabo.html.

Scott County Historical Society. sites.rootsweb.com/~vaschs2/superstitions1. htm.

Trent, Sydney. "Slavery Cost Him His Family. That's When Henry 'Box' Brown Mailed Himself to Freedom." *Washington Post*, December 28, 2019. www.washingtonpost.com/history/2019/12/28/slavery-cost-him-his-family-thats-when-henry-box-brown-mailed-himself-freedom.

University of Virginia. Division of Perceptual Studies. med.virginia.edu/ perceptual-studies/who-we-are/history-of-dops/dr-ian-stevenson.

Virginia Museum of History and Culture. www.virginiahistory.org/collections-and-resources/virginia-history-explorer/grace-sherwood-witch-pungo.

Virginia Places.org. www.virginiaplaces.org/rail.

White House. www.whitehouse.gov/about-the-white-house/first-families/ edith-bolling-galt-wilson.

ABOUT THE AUTHOR

Chuck Mills has a passion for history. He has roamed the world researching historical topics and is delighted to have lived most of his life in Northern Virginia, one of the most historic regions in the country. He now lives on the banks of the Potomac River on land once owned by George Washington.

Chuck is a graduate of Penn State University and has advanced degrees from Penn State and George Washington University. He recently completed a master's degree in American history at George Mason University in Fairfax, Virginia.

Chuck is a member of the Sons of the American Revolution, the Alexandria Historical Society, the Prince William Historic Preservation Society, a former member of the Board of Directors of the Manassas Museum and has acted as a docent at the Carlyle House Historic Park in Alexandria. He is the author of *Hidden History of Northern Virginia*, *Echoes of Manassas*, *Historic Cemeteries of Northern Virginia* and *Treasure Legends of the Civil War* and has written numerous newspaper and magazine articles on historical subjects. Chuck is the producer and co-host of *Virginia Time Travel*, a history television show that airs to some two million viewers in Northern Virginia.

When not doing genealogical or historical research, Chuck can be found kayaking on the Potomac River.